Spelling
Games and Activities

GRADE 5

All illustrations and photography, including those from Shutterstock.com, are protected by copyright.

Writing: Monika Davies
Content Editing: Kathleen Jorgensen
Lisa Vitarisi Mathews
Copy Editing: Cindie Farley
Art Direction: Yuki Meyer
Illustration: Bryan Langdo
Cover Design: Yuki Meyer
Design/Production: Paula Acojido
Yuki Meyer
Jessica Onken

EMC 8275

Congratulations on your purchase of some of the finest teaching materials in the world.

Photocopying the pages in this book is permitted for <u>single-classroom use only</u>. Making photocopies for additional classes or schools is prohibited.

For information about other Evan-Moor products, call 1-800-777-4362, fax 1-800-777-4332, or visit our website, www.evan-moor.com. Entire contents © 2023 Evan-Moor Corporation 10 Harris Court, Suite C-3, Monterey, CA 93940-5773. Printed in USA.

Contents

What's in *Spelling Games and Activities* 4

How to Use *Spelling Games and Activities* 7

Spelling Word List 8

Themed Units

Best Friends 11
    Words about friendship featuring words with suffixes

Mother Nature Rules! 21
    Words about Earth science featuring compound words;
    r-controlled words; and vowel digraphs **oo**, **ai**, and **ei**

It Takes All Kinds 31
    Words about different kinds of people featuring words with
    -er, **-or**, **-ist**, and **-est** suffixes

Seeing the World 41
    Words about travel featuring words with **-ture**, **-sure**, **-tion**,
    -sion, and **-age** suffixes

Friendly Competition 51
    Words about sports featuring compound words with consonant
    digraphs **sh**, **ch**, **ck**, and **ng** and vowel digraphs **oa**, **oe**, **ei**, **ie**,
    ee, **ou**, **ay**, and **ea**

Let's Go Out to Eat! 61
    Words about dining featuring multisyllable words, **r**-controlled
    words, and words with a silent **t**

Helping Others 71
    Words about helping others featuring hard and soft **c**; the
    schwa sound; and vowel digraphs **ee**, **ai**, **ie**, **ue**, and **au**

Wildlife 81
    Words about animals featuring **r**-controlled words; vowel
    digraphs **ee**, **ea**, **ou**, **ie**, and **eo**; and hard and soft **c**

Extra Practice Worksheets 91

Spelling Strategies 152

Answer Key 159

What's in Spelling Games and Activities

Support for Writing
Spelling skills are essential for children to practice in order to communicate well in writing. Many people rely on technology to fix their spelling, but technology can only guess what the writer means. Spelling must be accurate to be understood. Even though there are many spelling rules and even more exceptions, spelling practice can help students understand those rules and apply them to their writing.

Spelling Games and Activities gives you two ways to help your students practice spelling:

- the engaging themed unit section, which brings together related words in grade-appropriate contexts in fun and interesting ways
- the extra practice worksheets section, which uses words from Evan-Moor's *Building Spelling Skills* series and can be used to enrich those lessons or on its own

8 Themed Units
Spelling Games and Activities offers 8 units of grade-level topics that engage students and provide context for practicing spelling useful words. Each unit introduces 18 theme-related words along with the spelling patterns and rules that are used in those words. The unit continues with fun puzzles, cutouts, and other activities to practice writing and spelling the words, followed by a game or other special activity done as a class or in small groups.

Unit Features
You can assign all the pages in a cohesive unit or choose individual worksheets as needed to support your spelling program or to reinforce words learned in other content areas. Each 10-page unit provides a set of spelling words and related spelling tips, a variety of activity pages, and a game or project with teacher directions.

Unit Overview

An introduction telling students what the unit's words have in common, along with the words themselves

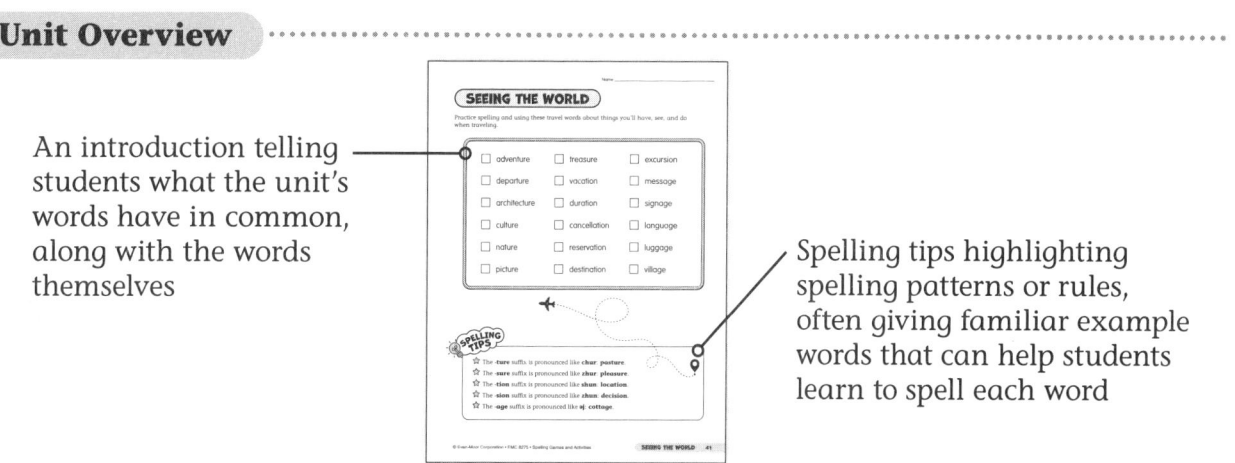

Spelling tips highlighting spelling patterns or rules, often giving familiar example words that can help students learn to spell each word

What's in Spelling Games and Activities, continued

Theme-Based Activity Pages

There are a wide variety of theme-based activities in every theme unit. These are some examples.

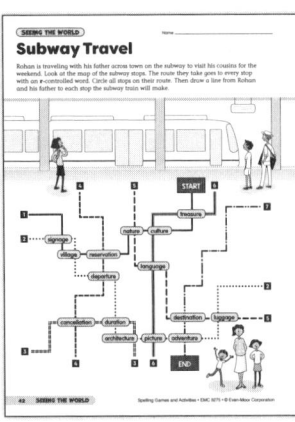
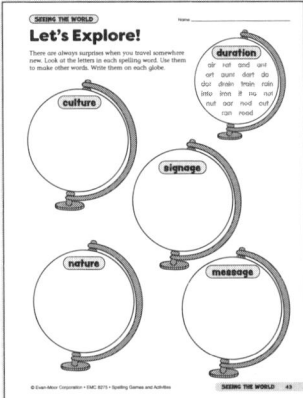

Connect similar words

Students analyze words, looking for specific spelling patterns or structures.

Make words from words

Students use the letters in their spelling words to make other words, discovering letter patterns along the way.

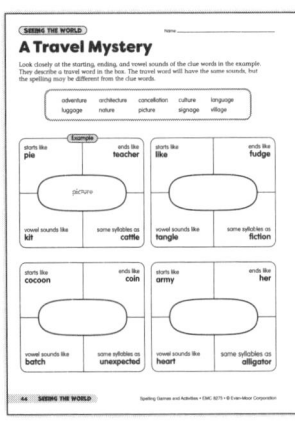

Find the mystery word

Students put together sound clues to figure out the mystery spelling word.

Find and fix misspellings

Students read short texts, identify mistakes, and fix them.

Game, Activity, or Hands-on Center

A fun theme-related game, often a variation of a familiar children's game, lets students practice their words in a small or large group setting.

A page of instructions and materials for the teacher is included, as well as any cards or game boards.

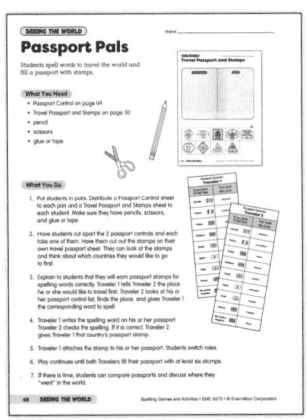
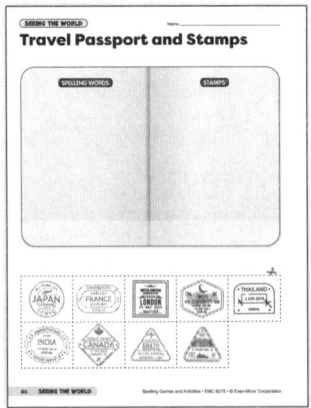

© Evan-Moor Corporation • EMC 8275 • Spelling Games and Activities

What's in Spelling Games and Activities, *continued*

Extra Practice Worksheets

Students apply the same spelling tips from the themed units to sets of words from *Building Spelling Skills*. These pages can be used independently or with any spelling series.

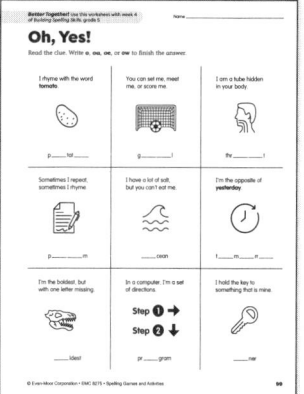
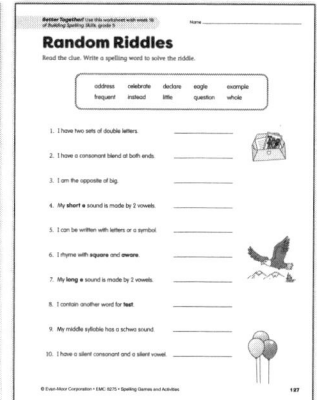

Additional Resources

Spelling Strategies

A variety of useful strategies that help students learn a word's spelling by analyzing sounds and word structures or by using dictionary skills and memory aids

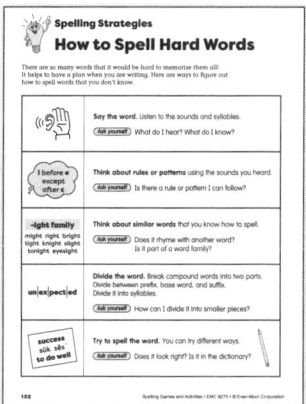
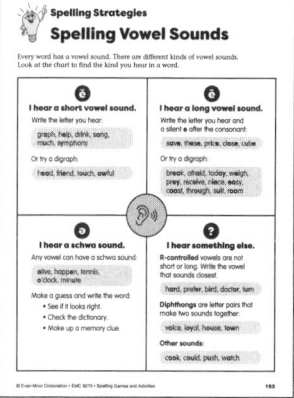
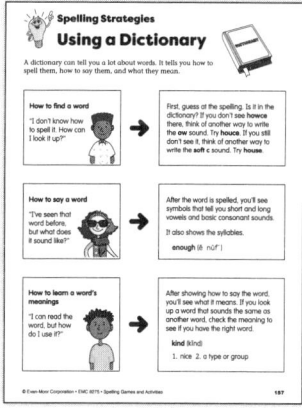

Spelling Word List

Alphabetized glossary of all spelling words in the book

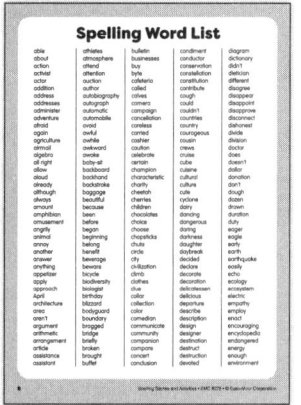

Answer Key

Provided for any page that has student answers. The correct answer or a sample response is shown, unless the question is completely open-ended.

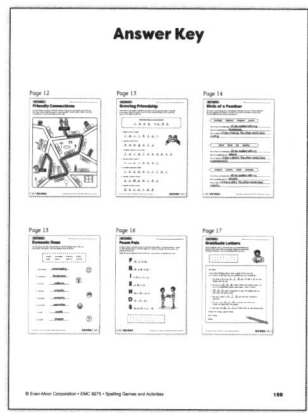

How to Use Spelling Games and Activities

Flexible Use

Decide which pages you will use. You can use an entire unit from the themed section, pages focusing on a particular skill, or extra practice pages that apply skills to different words. Then print copies for your students. It is recommended that you include the introduction page that provides helpful spelling tips for the skills you're working on.

Connections to Other Subjects

The units in this book were chosen to represent common experiences of children in fifth grade, along with general grade-level words. These topics may relate to other subjects you are teaching and could augment other lessons. For example, Helping Others could be used with an SEL lesson focusing on developing empathy. Seeing the World could be used with a social studies lesson. Mother Nature Rules! and Wildlife could extend a science lesson about weather or animal habitats. Friendly Competition could be used when students must spend recess inside on a rainy day. Use any set of spelling words with a handwriting lesson for extra practice in both.

Extend the Challenge or the Words

If you find an activity or game particularly useful, feel free to use it as a template for other sets of spelling words or other features of the same words. For example, the activity on page 142 asks students to sort words by the spelling of the **f** sound. You could change the words and have students do the same type of sort. You could also use the same words and ask them to sort by vowel sound or by spellings of the schwa sound.

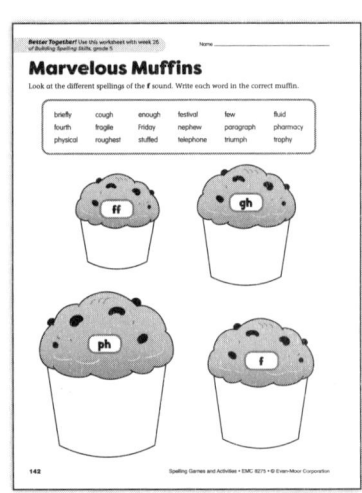

Use the Extra Practice Worksheets

If you want additional practice on specific skills or want students to practice applying skills to a new set of words, use pages from the extra practice section. This section features all the spelling words from Evan-Moor's *Building Spelling Skills* weekly lessons. If you are using *Building Spelling Skills*, you can use these extra practice worksheets to enhance your weekly lessons, giving students more practice with the same words.

Spelling Word List

able	athletes	bulletin	condiment	diagram
about	atmosphere	businesses	conductor	dictionary
action	attend	buy	conservation	didn't
activist	attention	byte	constellation	dietician
actor	auction	cafeteria	constitution	different
addition	author	called	contribute	disagree
address	autobiography	calves	cough	disappear
addresses	autograph	camera	could	disappoint
administer	automatic	campaign	couldn't	disapprove
adventure	automobile	cancellation	countries	disconnect
afraid	avoid	careless	country	dishonest
again	awful	carried	courageous	divide
agriculture	awhile	cashier	cousin	division
airmail	awkward	caution	crews	doctor
algebra	awoke	celebrate	cruise	does
all right	baby-sit	certain	cube	doesn't
allow	backboard	champion	cuisine	dollar
aloud	backhand	characteristic	cultural	donation
already	backstroke	charity	culture	don't
although	baggage	cheetah	cute	dough
always	beautiful	cherries	cyclone	dozen
amount	because	children	dairy	drawn
amphibian	been	chocolates	dancing	duration
amusement	before	choice	dangerous	duty
angrily	began	choose	daring	eager
animal	beginning	chopsticks	darkness	eagle
annoy	belong	chute	daughter	early
another	benefit	circle	daybreak	earth
answer	beverage	city	decided	earthquake
anything	beware	civilization	declare	easily
appetizer	bicycle	climb	decorate	echo
apply	biodiversity	clothes	decoration	ecology
approach	biologist	clue	delicatessen	ecosystem
April	birthday	collar	delicious	electric
architecture	blizzard	collection	departure	empathy
area	bodyguard	color	describe	employ
aren't	boundary	comedian	description	enact
argument	bragged	communicate	design	encouraging
arithmetic	bridge	community	designer	encyclopedia
arrangement	briefly	companion	destination	endangered
article	broken	compare	destruct	energy
assistance	brought	concert	destruction	enough
assistant	buffet	conclusion	devoted	environment

equation	friends	hour	lecture	nurturing
equator	friendship	house	legal	obey
eruption	fuel	humidity	length	occasion
especially	fundraiser	hurried	leopard	ocean
evacuation	future	idea	lessons	o'clock
everybody	generous	I'll	librarian	off
everyone	genius	illegal	license	office
exactly	geography	illegible	lightning	official
example	geologist	I'm	limb	oldest
exchange	geology	impatient	listen	once
excitement	geometry	imperfect	listener	one-way
exciting	glacier	impolite	little	only
excursion	gloomy	import	lives	orchestra
explain	goal	important	lonelier	ordinary
extinct	goalkeeper	improper	loneliness	organizer
faithful	good-bye	inactive	loose	other
families	gorilla	inconsiderate	loving	ounce
fault	gourmet	inconvenient	loyalty	ourselves
favorite	government	incorrect	luggage	outfield
fearless	governor	infection	lying	outside
fences	ground	infield	manager	owner
ferocious	grudge	inquire	manufacture	oxygen
festival	guarding	instead	marathon	oyster
few	guesses	instrument	maybe	paragraph
fiction	guitarist	integrity	mayor	partner
field	half	international	message	patience
fierce	hailstorm	intersection	meteorologist	payment
fifteen	hairstylist	island	misbehave	peaceful
figure	happen	isle	misfortune	pediatrician
finance	happily	isn't	mission	people
finished	happiness	it's	misspell	person
first aid	haul	I've	misunderstand	pharmacy
flashlight	haven't	January	misuse	photograph
flies	having	kindness	moisture	physical
fluid	healthiest	knapsack	monsoon	physician
followed	height	knew	months	picture
force	heir	knight	mountain	pictures
forecast	high school	knot	multiply	piece
forgiveness	higher	label	musician	planned
fourth	himself	laid	myself	playoff
fragile	hippopotamus	landscaper	nature	please
freestyle	homerun	language	neighborhood	pledge
freight	honestly	large	neither	plentiful
frequent	honesty	laughed	nephew	poem
Friday	honor	lawyer	nice	populate
friendly	horseshoes	leaves	nonprofit	population

portable	remember	smiling	thoughtful	unusual
position	representative	smuggler	thoughtless	urgent
potato	rescue	socialize	thousand	useless
precipitation	reservation	somehow	threatened	usually
predator	respectful	something	threw	utensils
predicament	restaurant	special	throat	vacation
prefix	rewrite	species	through	variety
prehistoric	rhinoceros	speedily	thumb	vegetarian
prejudice	rhyme	spoil	thunderstorm	vertical
prevent	rhythm	spoken	Thursday	very
preview	roofs	sprout	tidiest	village
principal	rookie	square	tiebreaker	volcano
principle	rough	stalk	tiniest	volunteer
professor	roughest	stare	tired	wasteful
program	route	station	together	watches
punctuate	royal	straight	tomorrow	weaker
punctuation	ruin	studied	tonight	weakness
puncture	sadness	stuffed	touchdown	weigh
punishment	safari	substitute	towel	weighs
purchases	sanctuary	successful	trace	weightlifting
purpose	sandstorm	sudden	trading	we're
python	savanna	sugar	transport	where
quarter	scene	supportive	traveling	whirlwind
quarterback	school	sure	treasure	whistle
question	scoreboard	surprise	tried	white
quickest	scratch	surrounded	triumph	whole
quiet	second	swimming	trophy	who's
quite	segment	sympathy	trouble	whose
racetrack	seismic	talking	truth	widest
radio	semicircle	teacher	truthful	wilderness
raise	several	technology	trying	women
ready	shoes	telegraph	tsunami	wonder
reappear	shortstop	telephone	Tuesday	wonderful
rebuild	should	telescope	two	won't
recall	siege	temperature	typhoon	worried
receipt	signage	tension	umpire	worries
receive	signal	terrible	unable	worthless
receiving	silent	their	unaware	wrestle
reckless	silliest	themselves	uncertain	write
recover	since	there's	uncomfortable	writing
referee	sincerity	they	understood	wrong
region	skiing	they're	ungrateful	wrote
regular	skillful	they've	unity	you're
reign	skis	thirsty	universe	
relation	skydiving	though	unknown	
relief	sleigh	thought	until	

Name _____

BEST FRIENDS

Practice spelling and using these words that are about what makes a good friend.

- ☐ respectful
- ☐ faithful
- ☐ encouraging
- ☐ generous
- ☐ courageous
- ☐ nurturing
- ☐ forgiveness
- ☐ devoted
- ☐ listener
- ☐ supportive
- ☐ patience
- ☐ empathy
- ☐ sympathy
- ☐ loyalty
- ☐ honesty
- ☐ unity
- ☐ sincerity
- ☐ integrity

SPELLING TIPS

☆ The suffix **-ful** is often used to make adjectives from nouns. Even though **-ful** means "full of," it is spelled with only one **l**. Examples: **joyful**, **thoughtful**

☆ Suffixes make a word longer and may look harder to spell, but you can divide the base word from the suffix and focus on spelling that part. Example: **sensitiv|ity**

☆ When adding a suffix that starts with a vowel to a base word that ends with an **e**, drop the **e** first. Example: **adventure̸ + -ous = adventurous**

If dropping the **e** changes the pronunciation of the base word, the **e** usually stays in. Example: **knowledge + -able = knowledgeable**

BEST FRIENDS   11

Friendly Connections

Mei and Evan are going to Deborah's house to hang out. Look at the map of the city bus stops. The bus they take goes to every stop with a 3-letter suffix. Draw a line from Mei and Evan to each stop their bus will make.

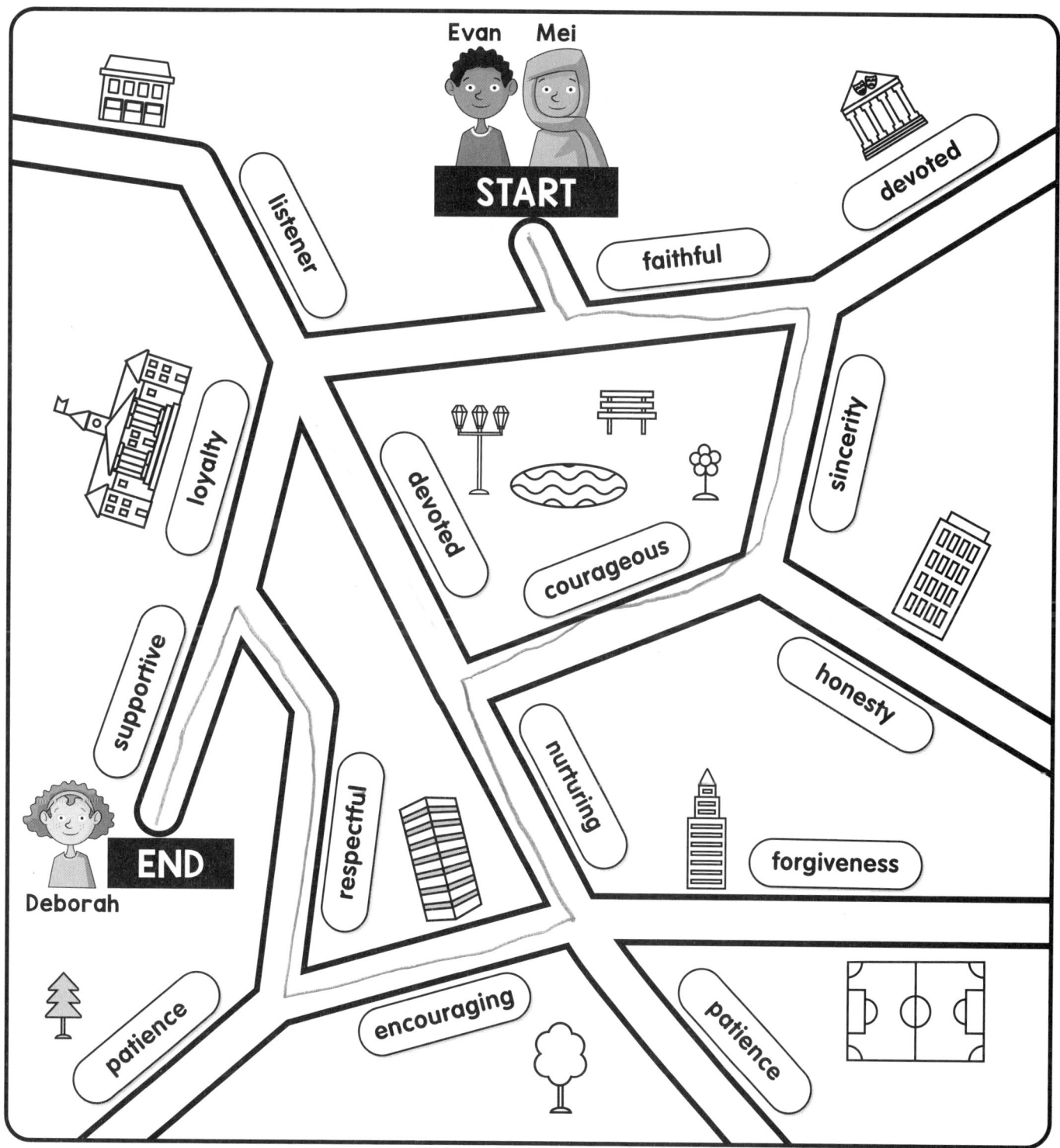

BEST FRIENDS

Growing Friendship

Name _____

One word in each group is spelled incorrectly. Find the word and spell it correctly in the spaces below the group. Then write the numbered letters in the matching spaces of the riddle to answer it.

What kind of flowers are best friends?

___ ___ ___ ___   b ___ ___ ___
 1   2   3   4   5   6   7

1. feithful, sincerity, integrity

   ___ ___ ___ ___ ___ ___ ___ ___
                              5

2. empathy, loyalty, honsty

   ___ ___ ___ ___ ___ ___ ___
               4

3. sensitivity, forgivness, encouraging

   ___ ___ ___ ___ ___ ___ ___ ___ ___ ___
       2

4. generous, listner, patience

   ___ ___ ___ ___ ___ ___ ___
                           1

5. respektful, supportive, faithful

   ___ ___ ___ ___ ___ ___ ___ ___ ___
           3

6. simpathy, generous, listener

   ___ ___ ___ ___ ___ ___ ___
   7

7. empathy, honesty, dovoted

   ___ ___ ___ ___ ___ ___ ___
           6

BEST FRIENDS

Name _____

Birds of a Feather

The words in each group have something in common, but one of them is different. Say each spelling word aloud to yourself. Then look at the letters in each word. Find the difference and answer the questions.

1. (encouraging   forgiveness   courageous   generous)

   How do these words **look** alike? _____

   Which one **sounds** different? _____

   How is it different? _____
   _____

2. (devoted   listener   unity   supportive)

   How do these words **look** alike? _____

   Which one **sounds** different? _____

   How is it different? _____
   _____

3. (courageous   respectful   sincerity   encouraging)

   How do these words **look** alike? _____

   Which one **sounds** different? _____

   How is it different? _____
   _____

BEST FRIENDS

Dynamic Duos

Name _____

You can change the silly phrases below to spell friendship words. After you unscramble each phrase, write the spelling word on the line.

> empathy   encouraging   forgiveness   integrity
> loyalty   patience   supportive   sympathy

1. rug canoeing _____

2. serving foes _____

3. tin peace _____

4. ham type _____

5. pay myths _____

6. pop virtues _____

7. toy ally _____

8. tiny tiger _____

© Evan-Moor Corporation • EMC 8275 • Spelling Games and Activities

Poem Pals

Katherine wrote an acrostic poem for her best friend, Hilmi. An acrostic poem is a poem in which the first letter of each line spells out a word or message. But the vowels went missing in this poem!

Finish the poem using the vowels in the box. Cross off each vowel after you use it.

F ___ ___ thf___ l

R ___ sp___ ctf___ l

I nt ___ gr ___ t ___

E mp ___ th ___

N ___ rt ___ r ___ ng

D ___ v ___ t ___ d

S ___ pp ___ rt ___ v ___

a	a	e	e	e	e	e	e	i	i	i
o	o	u	u	u	u	u	u	y	y	

BEST FRIENDS

Gratitude Letters

Mateo decided to write a gratitude letter to his best friend, Joey. Read his letter. Some letters are missing. Finish the words using the letters in the box. Cross off each letter after you use it.

```
e  e  e  g  h  i  n  o
o  p  p  r  r  s  t  t  u
```

Hey Joey,

I have been thinking about what a great friend you are.
So I wanted to tell you why I'm grateful for our friendship:

1. You have a lot of pa___ ___ ___ nce. I'm late a lot, but you always wait for me.

2. You are a s___ ___ ___ ortive friend. You always cheer me on at my basketball games, even when I miss a throw!

3. ___ ___ ___ esty is important to you. You always tell me the truth, no matter what.

4. You are a great li___ ___ ___ ner and ask thoughtful questions.

5. You are a gen___ ___ ___ us person and know how to pick out good gifts for people.

6. You have inte___ ___ ___ ty. That's what my dad always says!

Thanks for being a great friend.

Your buddy,

Mateo

(BEST FRIENDS)

Friendship Bingo

Students give each other clues to spell words on their bingo sheet.

What You Need

- Word Cards on page 19, enough to give each student 9 cards, cut out
- Bingo Sheet on page 20
- pencil

How to Play

The object of the game is to correctly write as many words as possible next to their descriptions.

1. Put students in pairs. Distribute a bingo sheet and 9 word cards to each student.

2. Explain to students that they will work with their partner using clues to write friendship words on their bingo sheets. Have students read the clues on their bingo sheets before they start the game to become familiar with the types of clues given. They will use these clues to decide where to write the words that they hear.

3. Player 1 chooses one of his or her word cards and reads aloud the spelling word and the clues. Player 2 finds a space with the same clues on his or her bingo sheet and writes the given word in that space, using the clues if needed. If using the Challenge Option below, Player 1 reads only the word and number of letters, not the second clue.

4. Students switch roles for the next turn.

5. The two students alternate until they use all their word cards. They trade bingo sheets and use the word cards to check that each word is spelled correctly and that the words are in the correct spaces.

6. If time allows, have students get their bingo sheet back and exchange word cards to play another round.

Challenge Option: If desired, Player 1 gives the word and the number of letters but not the second clue. Player 2 needs to decide which clue fits the word given in order to find the correct space.

BEST FRIENDS

Word Cards

Word unity	**Word** devoted	**Word** loyalty
Clues I have 5 letters. The last letter helps make the first sound.	**Clues** I have 7 letters. My first and last letter are the same.	**Clues** I have 7 letters. I have a vowel diphthong.

Word honesty	**Word** empathy	**Word** patience
Clues I have 7 letters. I start with a silent consonant.	**Clues** I have 7 letters. I have a consonant digraph.	**Clues** I have 8 letters. I have a silent **e**.

Word sympathy	**Word** listener	**Word** faithful
Clues I have 8 letters. One of my vowels has 2 different sounds.	**Clues** I have 8 letters. I have a silent consonant.	**Clues** I have 8 letters. My base word and suffix start with the same sound.

Word generous	**Word** nurturing	**Word** integrity
Clues I have 8 letters. I have a **soft g** sound.	**Clues** I have 9 letters. One of my consonants sounds like the digraph **ch**.	**Clues** I have 9 letters. I begin with a preposition.

Word sincerity	**Word** supportive	**Word** respectful
Clues I have 9 letters. I have a **soft c** sound.	**Clues** I have 10 letters. I have a double consonant.	**Clues** I have 10 letters. I have 3 consonants in a row.

Word courageous	**Word** encouraging	**Word** forgiveness
Clues I have 10 letters. I have two of the same vowel pair.	**Clues** I have 11 letters. I end in a 3-letter suffix.	**Clues** I have 11 letters. I have a silent **e** in the middle.

BEST FRIENDS

Bingo Sheet

Name _____

Word _____ **Clues** I have 5 letters. The last letter helps make the first sound.	**Word** _____ **Clues** I have 7 letters. My first and last letter are the same.	**Word** _____ **Clues** I have 7 letters. I have a vowel diphthong.
Word _____ **Clues** I have 7 letters. I start with a silent consonant.	**Word** _____ **Clues** I have 7 letters. I have a consonant digraph.	**Word** _____ **Clues** I have 8 letters. I have a silent **e**.
Word _____ **Clues** I have 8 letters. One of my vowels has 2 different sounds.	**Word** _____ **Clues** I have 8 letters. I have a silent consonant.	**Word** _____ **Clues** I have 8 letters. My base word and suffix start with the same sound.
Word _____ **Clues** I have 8 letters. I have a **soft g** sound.	**Word** _____ **Clues** I have 9 letters. One of my consonants sounds like the digraph **ch**.	**Word** _____ **Clues** I have 9 letters. I begin with a preposition.
Word _____ **Clues** I have 9 letters. I have a **soft c** sound.	**Word** _____ **Clues** I have 10 letters. I have a double consonant.	**Word** _____ **Clues** I have 10 letters. I have 3 consonants in a row.
Word _____ **Clues** I have 10 letters. I have two of the same vowel pair.	**Word** _____ **Clues** I have 11 letters. I end in a 3-letter suffix.	**Word** _____ **Clues** I have 11 letters. I have a silent **e** in the middle.

Name _____

MOTHER NATURE RULES!

Practice spelling and using these Earth science words about events on land and in the air.

- ☐ meteorologist
- ☐ blizzard
- ☐ monsoon
- ☐ forecast
- ☐ earthquake
- ☐ whirlwind
- ☐ tsunami
- ☐ lightning
- ☐ humidity
- ☐ thunderstorm
- ☐ hailstorm
- ☐ precipitation
- ☐ typhoon
- ☐ eruption
- ☐ evacuation
- ☐ volcano
- ☐ sandstorm
- ☐ seismic

SPELLING TIPS

★ Compound words are two words put together to make one word. Break up compound words into smaller words to make them easier to say and spell.
Example: **rainbow = rain + bow**

★ **R-controlled** vowels are any vowel followed by an **r**. The **r** changes the sound of the vowel. They sound different from long and short vowels.
Examples: nat**ur**al, wat**er**, wh**ir**lwind, vap**or**

★ Vowel digraphs are two vowels together that have one sound.
Examples: **oo**, **ai**, and **ei**: bl**oo**m, r**ai**n, h**ei**ght

MOTHER NATURE RULES!

Mother Earth

Name _____

What is the weather like? Read the word in each space.
Color each space following these rules:

- Use green for words with a **long i** sound.
- Use blue for compound words.
- Use gray for words with a suffix.
- Use brown for words that end in a vowel.

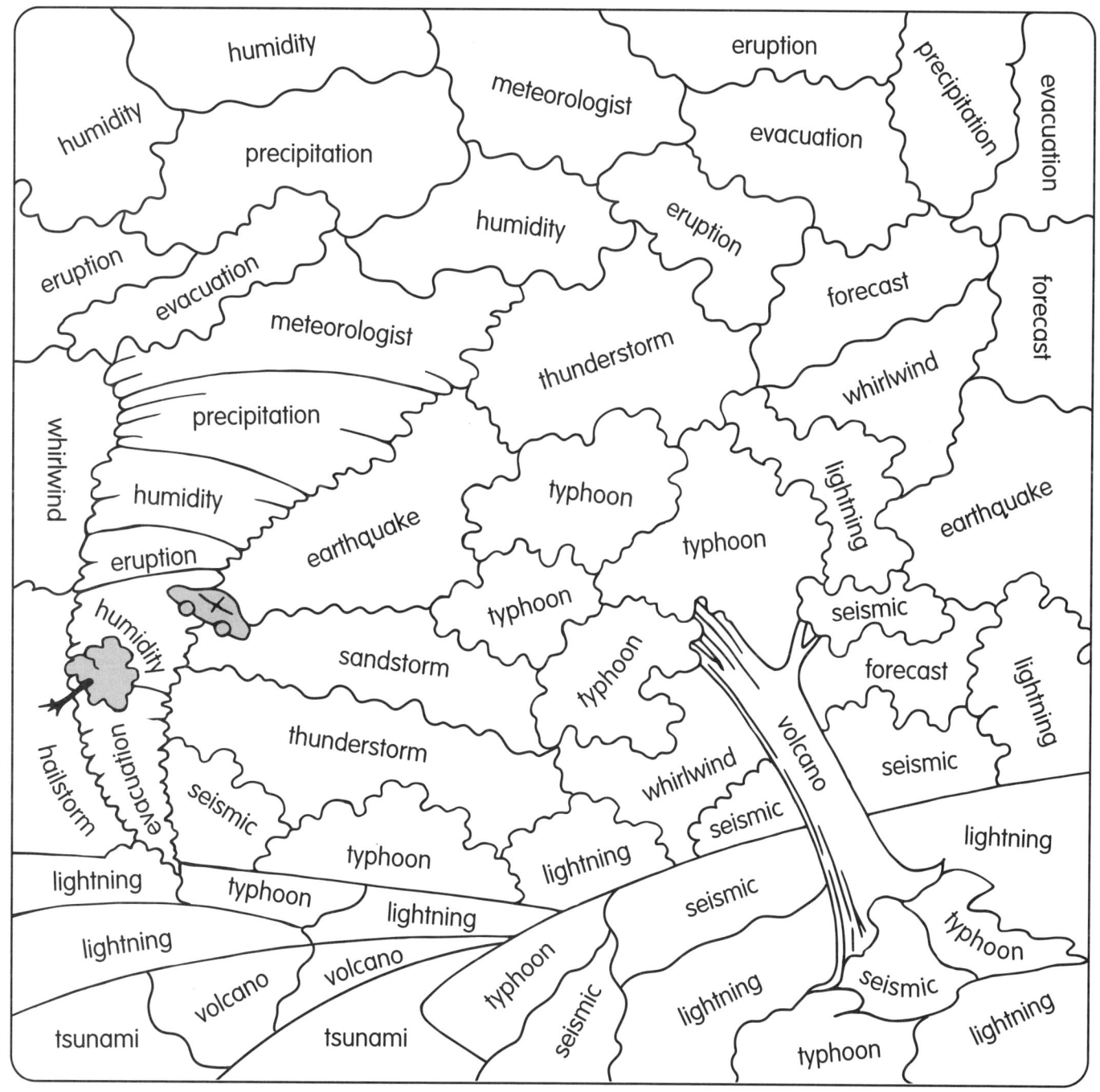

22 MOTHER NATURE RULES! Spelling Games and Activities • EMC 8275 • © Evan-Moor Corporation

MOTHER NATURE RULES!

Name _____

Make Mountains, Cut Canyons

Mountains are often formed when giant pieces of Earth's crust bump into each other hard enough to push land upward. Canyons are often formed when mountain snow melts into rivers that slowly wear away rock and cut the mountain in two.

Compound words are formed when words bump into each other. Each mountain below is home to a compound word. Draw a canyon to cut the word into two separate words. Write them in the box.

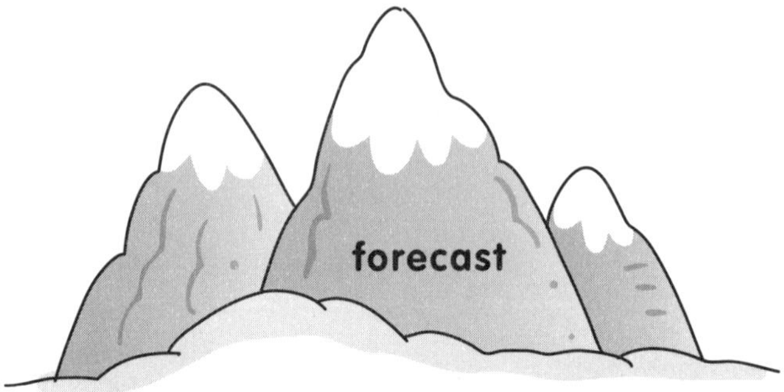

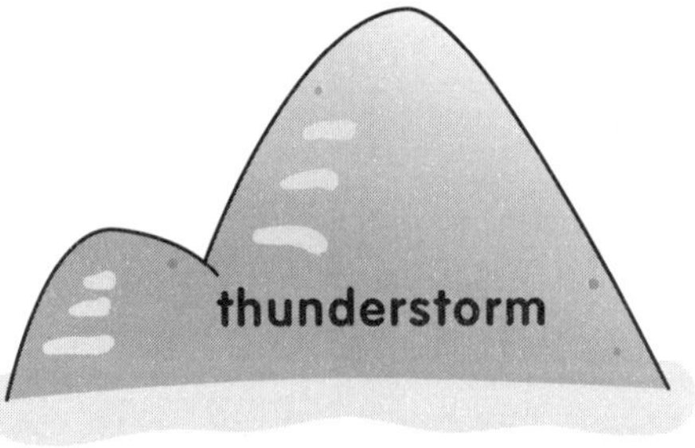

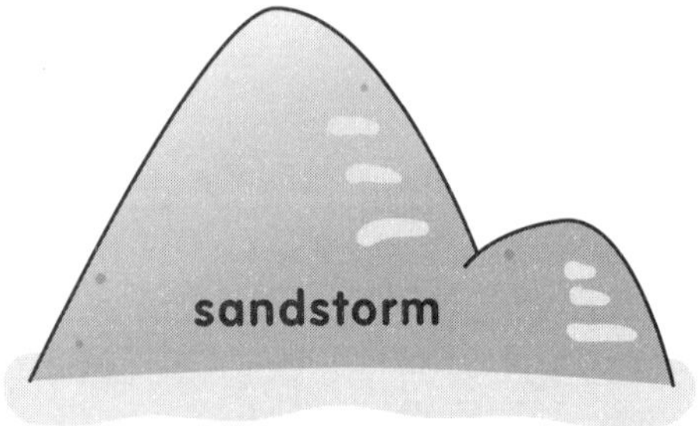

- earthquake
- forecast
- sandstorm
- thunderstorm
- hailstorm
- whirlwind

Separate words

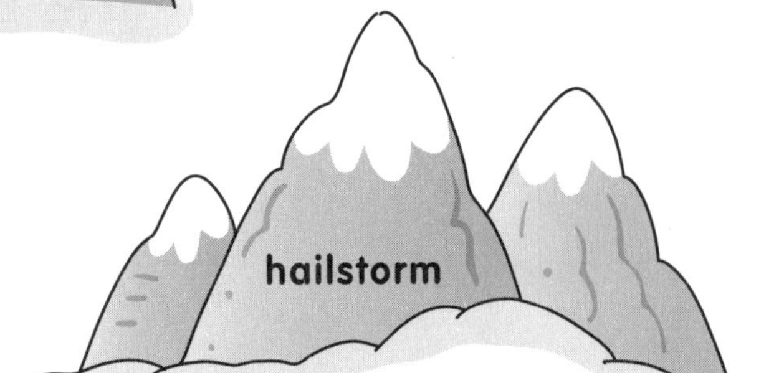

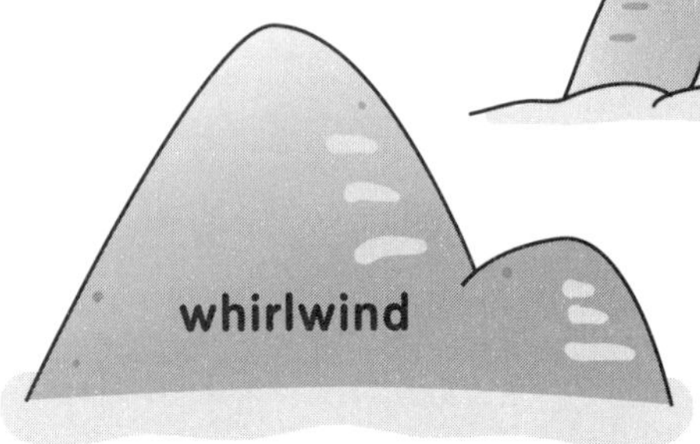

MOTHER NATURE RULES!

Close-up Clouds

Name _____

You never know what you might find inside a cloud: rain, sleet, or hail! Look at the letters in each spelling word. Use them to make other words. Write them on each cloud.

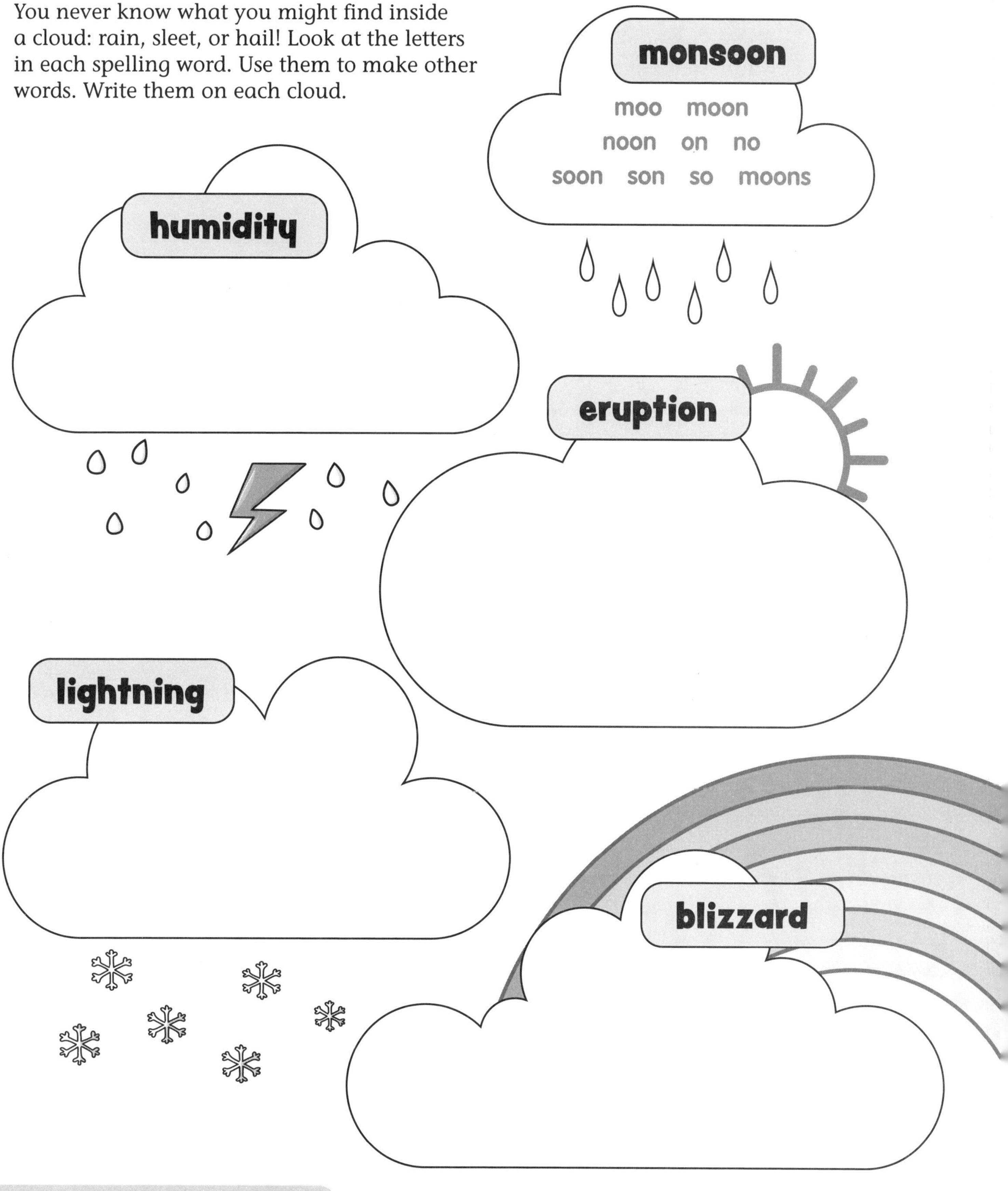

monsoon
moo moon
noon on no
soon son so moons

humidity

eruption

lightning

blizzard

MOTHER NATURE RULES!
Wild Riddles

Name _____

Read the clue. Write a spelling word to solve the riddle.

| earthquake | evacuation | meteorologist | precipitation | sandstorm |
| thunderstorm | tsunami | typhoon | volcano | whirlwind |

1. I look ahead to see what weather you can expect.

   _____
   (ends in **t**)

2. I spin and swirl and stir up danger wherever I go.

   _____
   (has 2 of the letter **w**)

3. When the weather wins, you'll do one of these.

   _____
   (ends in a 4-letter suffix)

4. I can be rain or sleet or hail or snow.

   _____
   (has 5 syllables)

5. When I "wave," people run away.

   _____
   (ends in **i**)

6. I bring a lot of noise with my rain.

   _____
   (has **r**-controlled vowels)

7. I rhyme with **shake** for a good reason.

   _____
   (compound word)

8. Watch out! I might blow my top.

   _____
   (ends in an **o** sound)

9. You will see me gusting around the desert.

   _____
   (has 2 of the letter **s**)

10. I rhyme with **tune**, but you can't dance to me.

    _____
    (has a vowel digraph)

MOTHER NATURE RULES!

Forces of Nature

Amari is making a poster with photos and captions about different natural events. Read the captions. Some letters are missing. Finish the words using the letters below. Cross off each letter after you use it.

This is an ____ ____ uption from a volcano. Look at the lava!

The f____ ____ cast told us that a hailst____ ____ m is on its way.

Mete____ ____ ologists can predict a blizz____ ____ d or thund____ rstorm.

Seismic scientists are working on ____ ____ thquake warning systems.

a a e e e e o
o o r r r r r r

MOTHER NATURE RULES!

Volcano Vowels

Name _____

The words below are missing their vowel digraphs! Luckily, there's a volcano erupting with vowels nearby.

Finish the words using the vowels on the volcano. Cross off each letter after you use it.

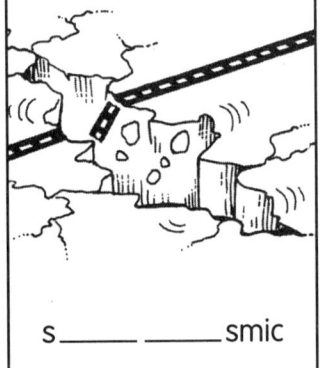
s_____smic

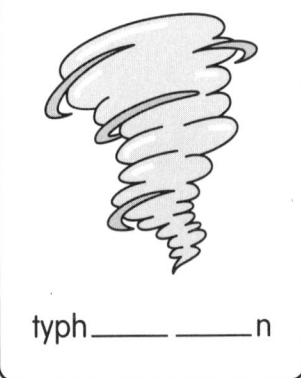
typh_____n

mons_____n

h_____lstorm

MOTHER NATURE RULES!

Wild-Weather Warning

Students work together to write and present their own wild-weather forecast using spelling words.

What You Need

- Words and Sentence Starters on page 29
- Wild-Weather Warning on page 30
- pencil
- art supplies or devices to make a visual display (optional)

What You Do

1. Put students in pairs. Distribute the Words and Sentence Starters to each student and the Wild-Weather Warning to each pair of students.

2. Explain to students that they will act as a meteorologist. They will work together to write a forecast including a weather warning to let people know about some upcoming dangerous weather where you live or in a fictional area. A "weather warning" is an alert to let citizens know about unsafe weather conditions.

3. Have students look at the Words and Sentence Starters sheet. Have partners discuss which spelling words they will use.

4. Have students use at least five spelling words to write a forecast and weather warning on the Wild-Weather Warning sheet. They can create any visual displays as well, if desired; distribute art supplies or devices as needed. Have students decide who will say which part and practice presenting it.

5. Have students present their forecasts and weather warnings to the class.

(MOTHER NATURE RULES!) Name _____

Words and Sentence Starters

Include at least five of these words in your forecast and weather warning:

blizzard	earthquake	eruption	evacuation	forecast
humidity	lightning	meteorologist	monsoon	sandstorm
seismic	tsunami	typhoon	volcano	whirlwind

 Tips for writing:

- Introduce yourselves.
- Let people know what kind of weather to expect in the upcoming week.
- Suggest activities to help people remain calm. For example, you could let people know that they should stay inside when there is dangerous weather outside.

Forecast sentence starters:

Hi there! My name is _____, and this is _____.

We are _____, who want to tell you about the weather this week.

It's going to be a wild-weather week! On Monday, there is a high chance of

_____ happening.

Don't forget—when _____ happens, it's very important to…

© Evan-Moor Corporation • EMC 8275 • Spelling Games and Activities   MOTHER NATURE RULES!   29

MOTHER NATURE RULES!

Wild-Weather Warning

Name _____

Name _____

An important update from the desks of

_____ and _____

_____
_____
_____
_____
_____
_____
_____
_____
_____
_____
_____
_____
_____
_____
_____
_____
_____

IT TAKES ALL KINDS

Practice spelling and using these words that describe someone or name someone who does something.

- ☐ champion
- ☐ companion
- ☐ librarian
- ☐ comedian
- ☐ dietician
- ☐ pediatrician
- ☐ conductor
- ☐ governor
- ☐ professor
- ☐ manager
- ☐ designer
- ☐ landscaper
- ☐ guitarist
- ☐ hairstylist
- ☐ activist
- ☐ healthiest
- ☐ silliest
- ☐ tidiest

SPELLING TIPS

★ The suffix **-or** is often used to make "doer" words from verbs ending in **-ate**, **-ct**, and **-it**. Examples: **investigator**, **contractor**, **visitor**

★ The suffix **-er** is often used to make "doer" words from verbs with other endings, especially a silent **e** or a consonant pair. Examples: **baker**, **singer**

★ The suffix **-ist** is often used with nouns, especially beliefs and people who play musical instruments. Some jobs also use this suffix. Examples: **pacifist**, **pianist**, **dentist**

★ The suffix **-est** makes an adjective meaning "most." Example: **easiest**

IT TAKES ALL KINDS
New Job

Name _____

Jagmeet's band is going to play. He will go through the "doer" words that end in **-ian**, **-er**, and **-ist**. Draw a line to make a path for Jagmeet to reach the rest of his band.

START

	healthiest	comedian	guitarist	landscaper
activist	champion	designer	silliest	dietician
librarian	manager	hairstylist	governor	designer
professor	silliest	tidiest	manager	hairstylist
champion	designer	pediatrician	activist	conductor
silliest	librarian	governor	companion	professor
companion	guitarist	landscaper	dietician	END

32 IT TAKES ALL KINDS   Spelling Games and Activities • EMC 8275 • © Evan-Moor Corporation

IT TAKES ALL KINDS

Yearbook Visions

The yearbook predicts what each student will do. Read the captions. Some suffixes are missing. Finish the words using the letters in the box. Cross off each letter as you use it.

a	a	e	e	i	i
n	n	r	s	s	t	t

MOST LIKELY TO...

... read over 1,000 books and become a librar _____ .

... be a manag _____ in a large tech corporation.

... be the silli _____ comed _____ on the stage.

... design the tidi _____ closet spaces in fancy homes.

IT TAKES ALL KINDS

Yearbook Visions, continued

a a e i i i i n n n o s t t

MOST LIKELY TO...

... become an Olympic champ _____.

... take care of kids as a pediatric _____.

... travel the world as a famous violin _____.

... help people make the healthi _____ food choices as a dietic _____.

IT TAKES ALL KINDS

Now Hiring!

Look at this page from a Job Ads website. Write a word from the box to complete each ad.

| comedian | companion | guitarist | hairstylist |
| healthiest | landscaper | manager | tidiest |

1. We're hiring a _____!

   We are looking for kind and respectful people to spend time with our senior citizens. Our center is known for being one of the _____ retirement communities. Join us!

2. Our salon is looking for a _____.

   We are looking for someone who can work part-time and keeps up on the latest looks. You may move up to be a _____ and run the salon someday.

3. _____ wanted!

   Are you ready to make music with us? Our band is looking for a bandmate who can rock and roll with us. Bonus points if you are a _____ and can make us laugh!

4. Are you a _____?

   Our lawn-care company has over 30 customers. We need someone to mow lawns. If you love a well-kept yard and are one of the _____ people you know, please apply.

Vision Board

IT TAKES ALL KINDS

Name _____

Harper is making a vision board to plan for her future! Circle any misspelled words. Write them correctly below.

DREAMS
To be a kind and vocal activst for others!

INSPIRATION
My mom inspires me to take care of others. She's a pedtrician!

I WANT TO TRY
I want to try to be the siliest person in my grade and make people laugh!

INSPIRATION
Simone Biles inspires me! She's an Olympic campion who focuses on her mental health.

GOALS
I want to become the govnor of my state someday.

Correctly spelled words:

_____ _____ _____

_____ _____

Career Changes

You can change the silly phrases below to spell a career word. After you unscramble each phrase, write the spelling word on the line.

> activist   companion   conductor   designer
> hairstylist   landscaper   librarian   professor

1. cedar plans   _____

2. roof press   _____

3. brain rail   _____

4. thirty sails   _____

5. cat visit   _____

6. cord count   _____

7. see grind   _____

8. onion camp   _____

IT TAKES ALL KINDS
Fill-in-a-Future

Name _____

Students work in pairs to "predict" their future career path by completing a silly story using their spelling words.

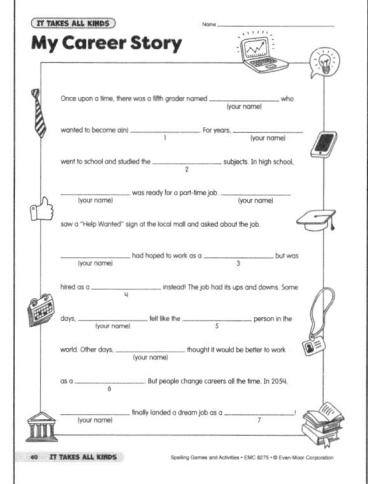

What You Need
- Dice Options on page 39
- My Career Story on page 40
- die
- pencil

What You Do

1. Put students in pairs. Distribute a die and a Dice Options sheet to each pair and a My Career Story sheet to each student.

2. Have students write their first name in all the blank spaces above "your name" on their My Career Story sheet.

3. Explain to students that they will be filling in blanks in a story by rolling a die.

4. Player 1 in each pair keeps his or her My Career Story sheet, the die, and a pencil. Player 2 has the Dice Options sheet.

    - Player 1 finds the first numbered blank space, rolls the die, and calls out the number rolled.
    - Player 2 finds the column for the number rolled on the Dice Options sheet, looks down to the row for blank space 1, and tells Player 1 the word.
    - Player 1 writes the word in blank space 1 on the My Career Story sheet.

5. Players repeat for all the numbered blank spaces in the story. Then Player 1 reads his or her story aloud.

6. Players switch roles and repeat.

7. If there is time, invite some students to share their career stories with the class.

38 IT TAKES ALL KINDS   Spelling Games and Activities • EMC 8275 • © Evan-Moor Corporation

IT TAKES ALL KINDS

Dice Options

Blank Space Number	Spelling Words		
	⚀ or ⚃	⚁ or ⚄	⚂ or ⚅
1	comedian	governor	companion
2	healthiest	silliest	tidiest
3	professor	conductor	guitarist
4	librarian	champion	dietician
5	silliest	tidiest	healthiest
6	landscaper	activist	manager
7	hairstylist	designer	pediatrician

My Career Story

IT TAKES ALL KINDS

Name _____

Once upon a time, there was a fifth grader named _____, who
(your name)

wanted to become a(n) _____. For years, _____
　　　　　　　　　　　　　1　　　　　　　　　　　　　　(your name)

went to school and studied the _____ subjects. In high school,
　　　　　　　　　　　　　　　　2

_____ was ready for a part-time job. _____
(your name)　　　　　　　　　　　　　　　　　　　(your name)

saw a "Help Wanted" sign at the local mall and asked about the job.

_____ had hoped to work as a _____ but was
(your name)　　　　　　　　　　　　　　　　　3

hired as a _____ instead! The job had its ups and downs. Some
　　　　　　　4

days, _____ felt like the _____ person in the
　　　　(your name)　　　　　　　　　　　5

world. Other days, _____ thought it would be better to work
　　　　　　　　　　(your name)

as a _____. But people change careers all the time. In 2054,
　　　　6

_____ finally landed a dream job as a _____!
(your name)　　　　　　　　　　　　　　　　　　　　　　　7

40　IT TAKES ALL KINDS

SEEING THE WORLD

Practice spelling and using these travel words about things you'll have, see, and do when traveling.

☐ adventure   ☐ treasure   ☐ excursion
☐ departure   ☐ vacation   ☐ message
☐ architecture ☐ duration   ☐ signage
☐ culture   ☐ cancellation ☐ language
☐ nature   ☐ reservation   ☐ luggage
☐ picture   ☐ destination   ☐ village

SPELLING TIPS

★ The **-ture** suffix is pronounced like **chur**: **pasture**.
★ The **-sure** suffix is pronounced like **zhur**: **pleasure**.
★ The **-tion** suffix is pronounced like **shun**: **location**.
★ The **-sion** suffix is pronounced like **zhun**: **decision**.
★ The **-age** suffix is pronounced like **əj**: **cottage**.

Subway Travel

Rohan is traveling with his father across town on the subway to visit his cousins for the weekend. Look at the map of the subway stops. The route they take goes to every stop with an **r**-controlled word. Circle all stops on their route. Then draw a line from Rohan and his father to each stop the subway train will make.

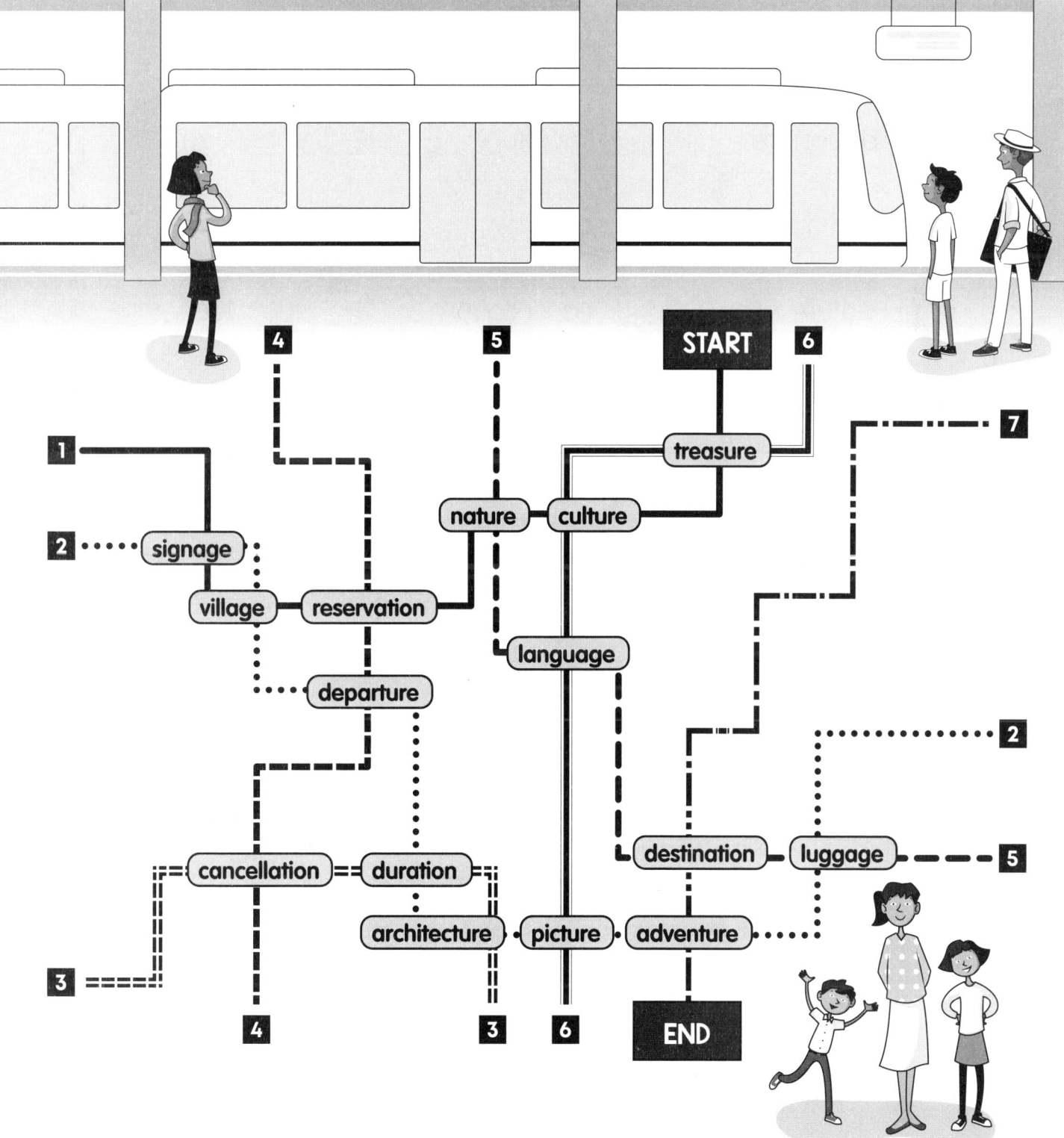

Let's Explore!

SEEING THE WORLD

Name _____

There are always surprises when you travel somewhere new. Look at the letters in each spelling word. Use them to make other words. Write them on each globe.

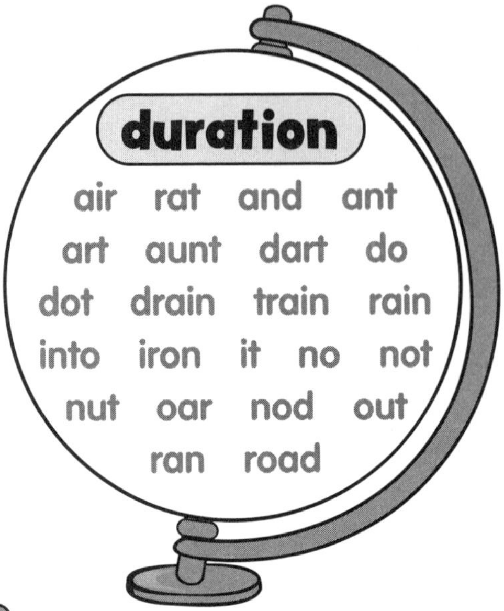

duration

air   rat   and   ant
art   aunt   dart   do
dot   drain   train   rain
into   iron   it   no   not
nut   oar   nod   out
ran   road

culture

signage

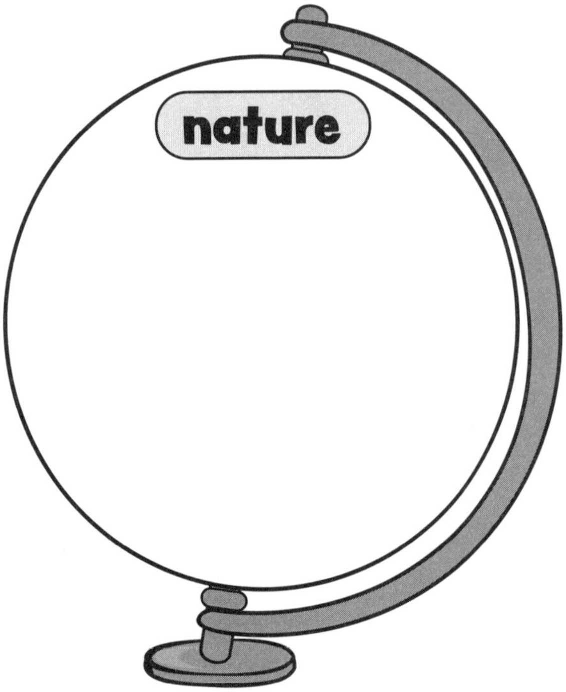

nature

message

SEEING THE WORLD

Name _____

A Travel Mystery

Look closely at the starting, ending, and vowel sounds of the clue words in the example. They describe a travel word in the box. The travel word will have the same sounds, but the spelling may be different from the clue words.

| adventure | architecture | cancellation | culture | language |
| luggage | nature | picture | signage | village |

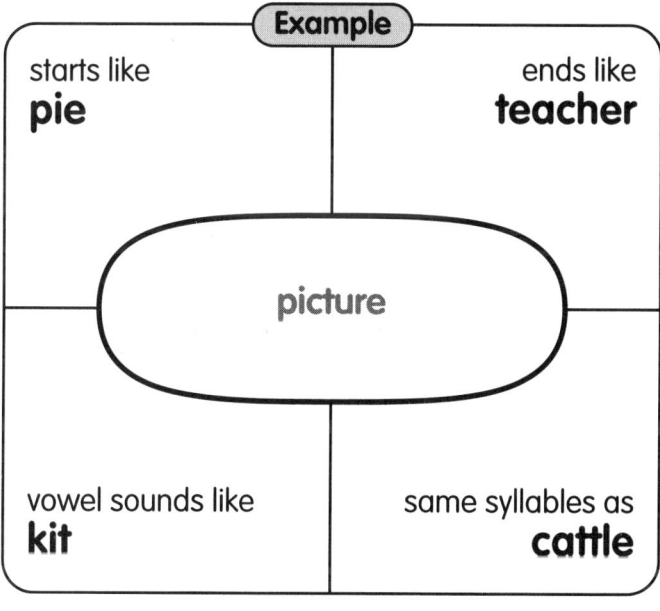

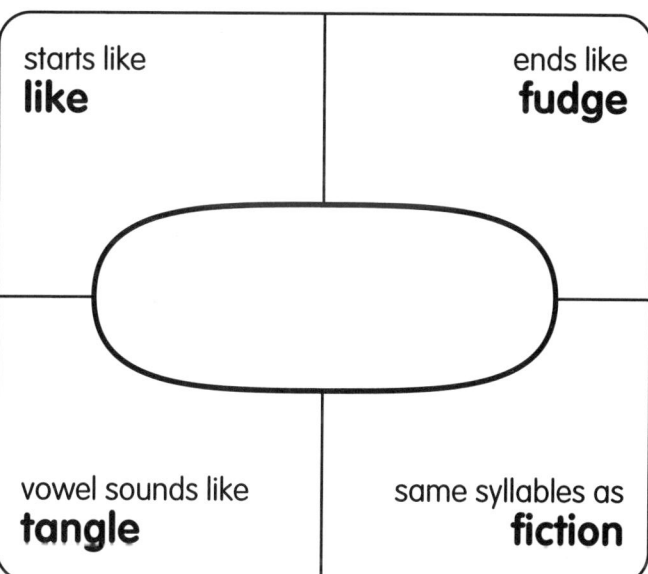

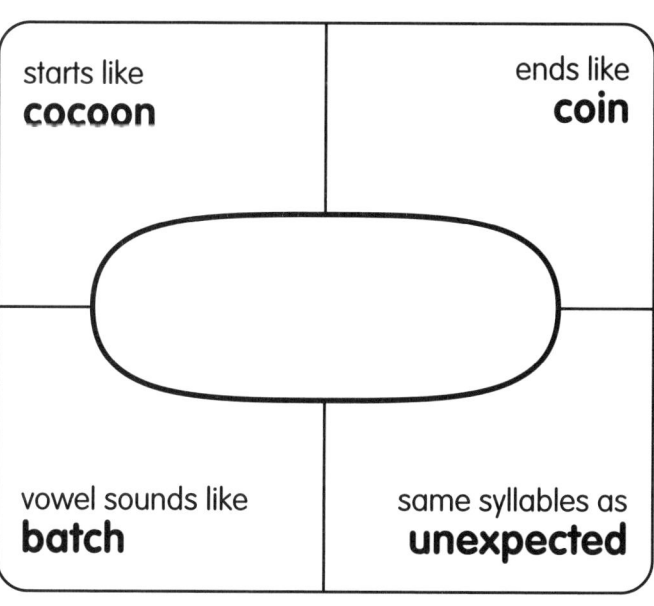

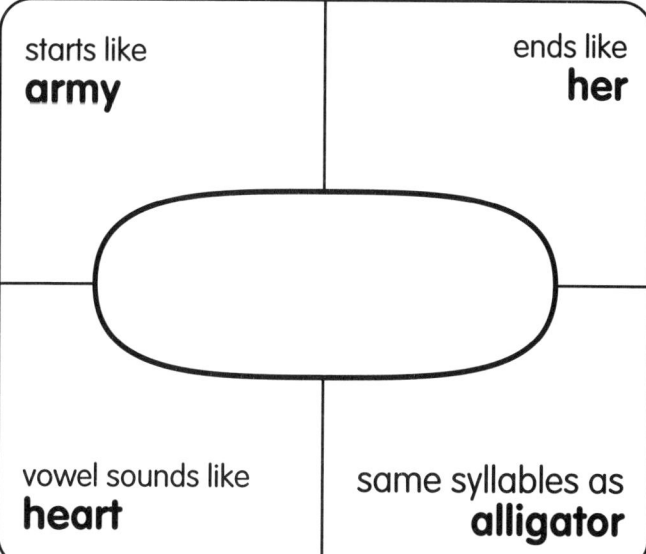

44 SEEING THE WORLD Spelling Games and Activities • EMC 8275 • © Evan-Moor Corporation

(SEEING THE WORLD)

Travel Checklist

Name _____

Javier and his family are going on their first overseas trip. Look at Javier's travel checklist. Some of the vowels fell off the list! Luckily, there are extra vowels packed away.

Finish the words using the vowels in the suitcase. Cross off each vowel after you use it.

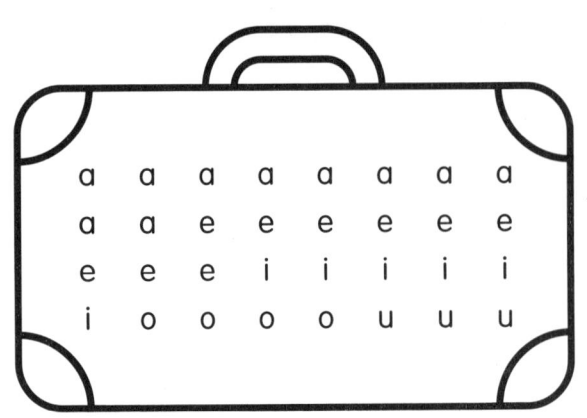

☐ Check our d __ p __ rt __ r __ time from the airport.

☐ Let our neighbors know the d __ r __ t __ __ n of our trip.

☐ Look up the c __ nc __ ll __ t __ __ n policy for our hotel in Rome.

☐ Print out the res __ rv __ t __ __ n e-mail for each d __ st __ n __ t __ __ n on our trip.

☐ Send a m __ ss __ g __ to our travel agent to check our tour times.

☐ Learn how to say "hello" and "thank you" in the Italian l __ ng __ __ g __.

☐ Get a map to my uncle's v __ ll __ g __.

© Evan-Moor Corporation • EMC 8275 • Spelling Games and Activities

SEEING THE WORLD

Rave Reviews

Visitors often write reviews for places they see while traveling. Read each review. Circle any misspelled words. Write them correctly below.

Parminder ⭐⭐⭐⭐⭐ 2 months ago

This palace is an astonishing piece of arketecture. This was our first vaycation as a family. Everyone, even my 8-year-old son, was impressed.

_____

Matilda ⭐⭐⭐⭐⭐ 3 weeks ago

We made a resurvation so we would not have to wait in line to go up in the tower. Be aware that there is no place to put your luggag there. We give this excurtion 5 stars!

_____

Noah ⭐⭐⭐⭐⭐ 5 days ago

New York City has always been a dream distenation. It has some of the tallest buildings in the world! We had an advantere riding a ferry boat. We took piktures of the city lit up at night. Don't miss seeing this treshure!

_____

SEEING THE WORLD

Stay in Touch

Beth lives in Seoul, the capital of South Korea. She writes to her mother in Connecticut every Sunday. Read her e-mail. The underlined words are scrambled. Write the words correctly above each one.

Name _____

culture   departure   destination
excursion   language   nature
picture   signage   vacation
village

New message

To: Mama Bear

Subject: Hello from South Korea!

Hi Mom!

Thanks for the icrpetu of Snickerdoodle. Our puppy is so big now!

I'm slowly getting used to the ulrcetu here in Seoul. The Korean anglaueg is hard to learn. But I can read the iggsena in my city now!

Last week, I got out into ntearu. Everyone told me that Yongin was a dtseoinnait that I must see. The folk vgillae is a great place to learn about Korean history. It was an onrucixes that I'll never forget!

I'm so happy that you're taking your ciantavo here! What is your reetrudpa date? I'm excited to show you around! I miss you a lot.

Love,

Beth

Send

SEEING THE WORLD
Passport Pals

Name _____

Students spell words to travel the world and fill a passport with stamps.

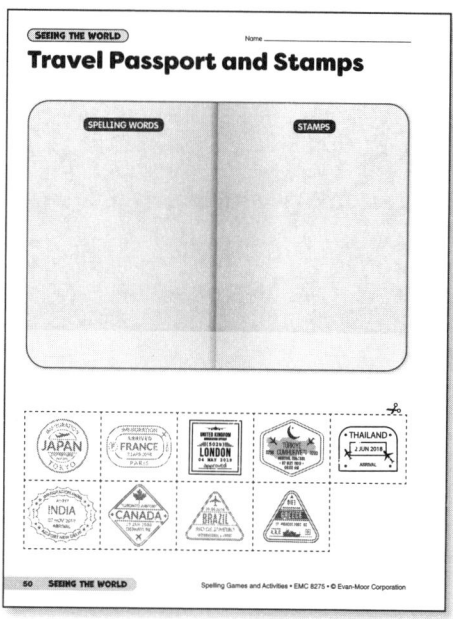

What You Need
- Passport Control on page 49
- Travel Passport and Stamps on page 50
- pencil
- scissors
- glue or tape

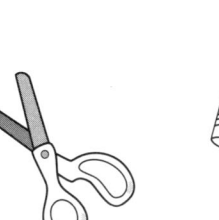

What You Do

1. Put students in pairs. Distribute a Passport Control sheet to each pair and a Travel Passport and Stamps sheet to each student. Make sure they have pencils, scissors, and glue or tape.

2. Have students cut apart the 2 passport controls and each take one of them. Have them cut out the stamps on their own travel passport sheet. They can look at the stamps and think about which countries they would like to go to first.

3. Explain to students that they will earn passport stamps for spelling words correctly. Traveler 1 tells Traveler 2 the place he or she would like to travel first. Traveler 2 looks at his or her passport control list, finds the place, and gives Traveler 1 the corresponding word to spell.

4. Traveler 1 writes the spelling word on his or her passport. Traveler 2 checks the spelling. If it is correct, Traveler 2 gives Traveler 1 that country's passport stamp.

5. Traveler 1 attaches the stamp to his or her passport. Students switch roles.

6. Play continues until both Travelers fill their passport with at least six stamps.

7. If there is time, students can compare passports and discuss where they "went" in the world.

SEEING THE WORLD
Passport Control

Passport Control: Traveler 1		Passport Control: Traveler 2	
If you want to visit here	**Then spell this word**	**If you want to visit here**	**Then spell this word**
Canada	adventure	Canada	departure
France	architecture	France	cancellation
Turkey	culture	Turkey	nature
Thailand	picture	Thailand	treasure
Brazil	vacation	Brazil	duration
Japan	reservation	Japan	destination
India	message	India	signage
Greece	language	Greece	luggage
The United Kingdom	excursion	The United Kingdom	village

© Evan-Moor Corporation • EMC 8275 • Spelling Games and Activities

Seeing the World
Travel Passport and Stamps

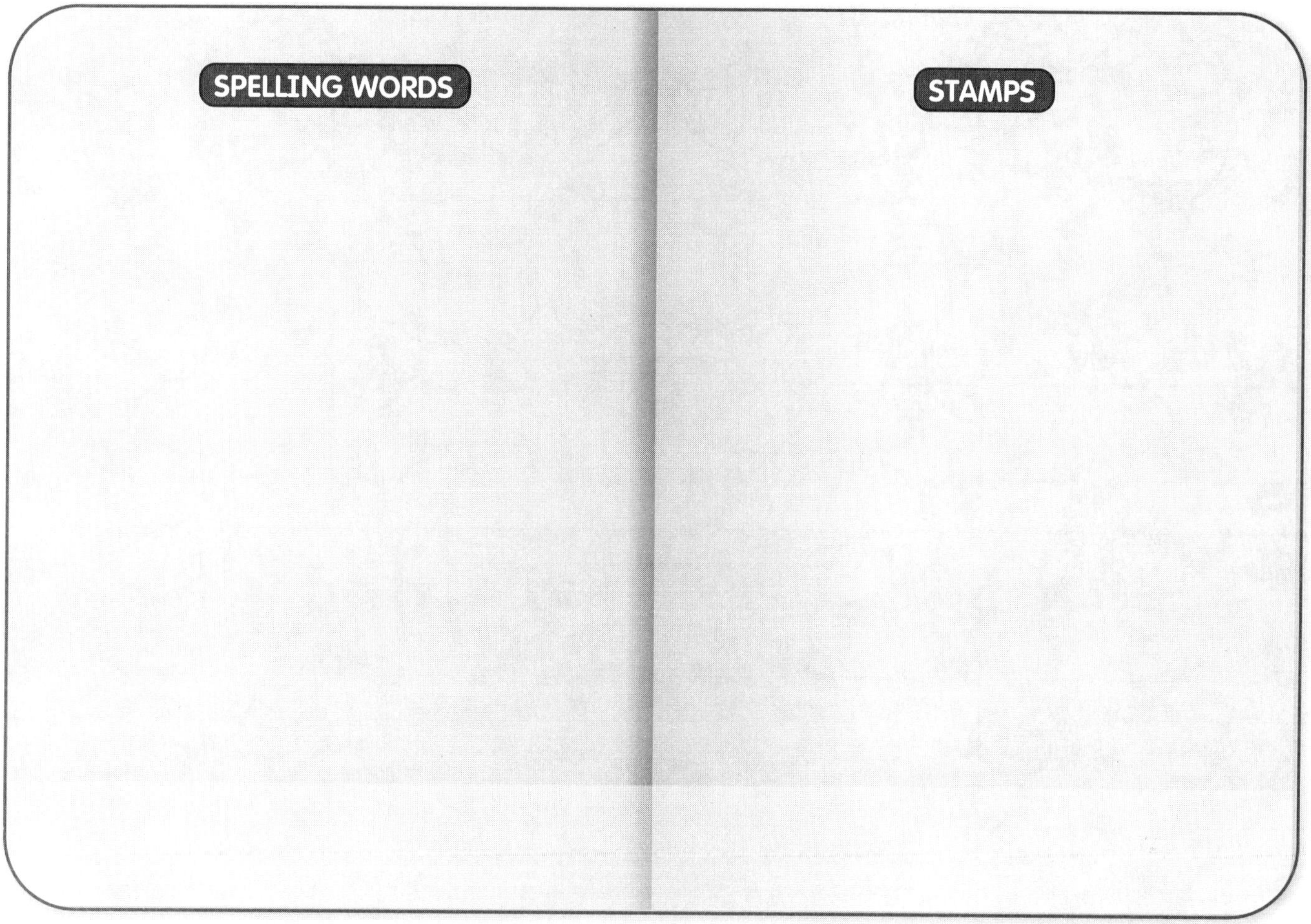

Name _____

SPELLING WORDS   **STAMPS**

FRIENDLY COMPETITION

Practice spelling and using these sports words about equipment, team positions, and competition places.

- ☐ horseshoes
- ☐ racetrack
- ☐ quarterback
- ☐ skydiving
- ☐ infield
- ☐ touchdown
- ☐ weightlifting
- ☐ outfield
- ☐ homerun
- ☐ backstroke
- ☐ backboard
- ☐ playoff
- ☐ freestyle
- ☐ shortstop
- ☐ tiebreaker
- ☐ backhand
- ☐ goalkeeper
- ☐ scoreboard

Spelling Tips

★ Consonant digraphs are two consonants that have one sound. Examples include **sh**, **ch**, **ck**, **ng**. Examples: **shoe**, **chase**, **puck**, **diving**

★ Vowel digraphs are two vowels that have one sound. Sometimes the sound is the same as one of the letters. Examples include **oa** and **ie**: **coach**, **field**.

★ Compound words are two words put together to make one word. Break up compound words into smaller words to make them easier to say and spell: **downhill = down + hill**.

★ The spelling rule "**i** before **e** except after **c**" is true in many cases, but there are exceptions. For example, when the vowel digraph sounds like a **long a**, the **e** comes before the **i**. Example: **weigh**

The Winning Basket

FRIENDLY COMPETITION

Name _____

Malika will score the winning basket. She will go through the words that contain the **sh** or **ck** consonant digraphs or the **oa** vowel digraph. Draw a line to show Malika's path down to the basket.

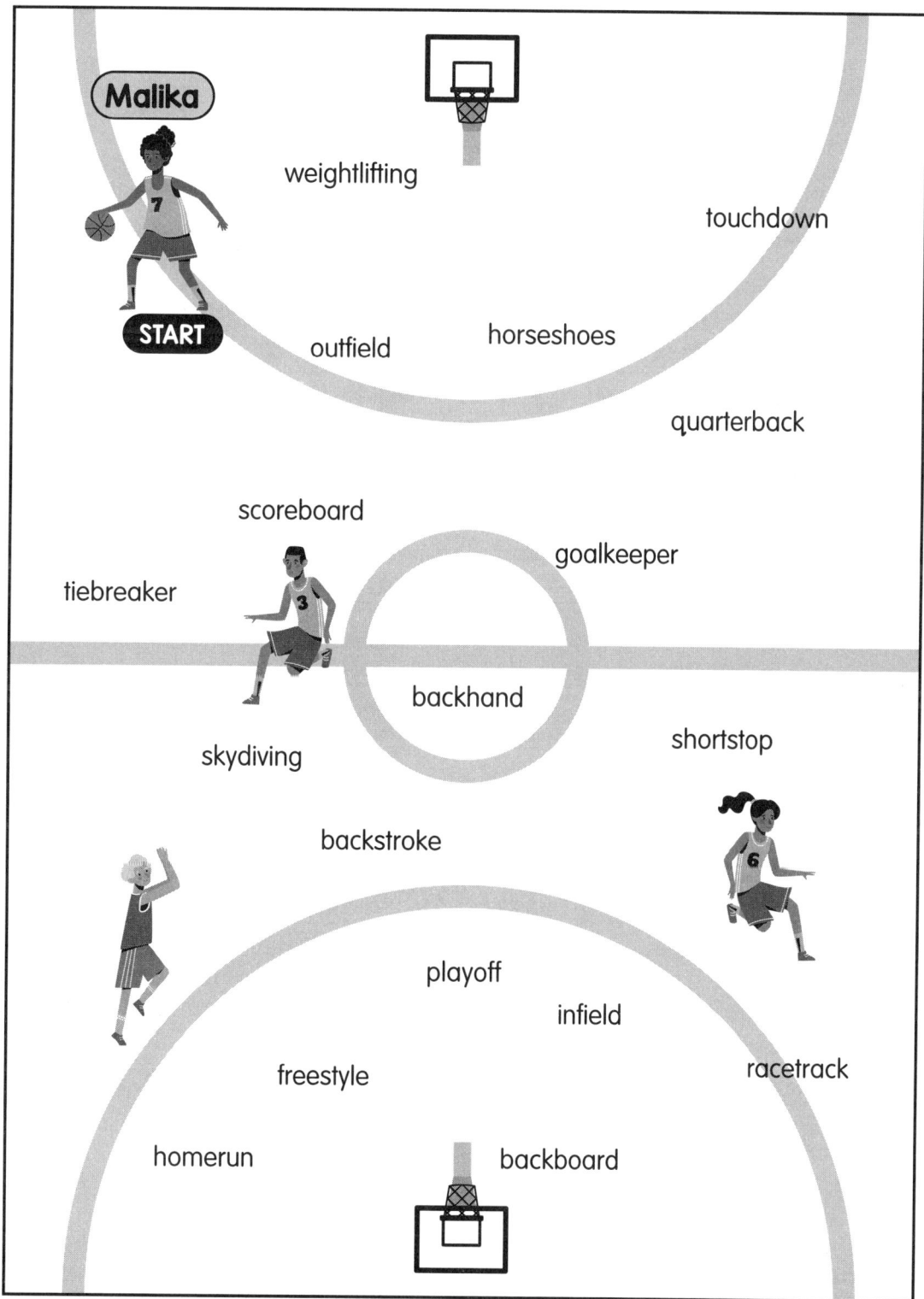

Baseball Brainteaser

FRIENDLY COMPETITION

Name _____

One word in each group is spelled incorrectly. Find the word and spell it correctly in the spaces below the group. Then write the numbered letters in the matching spaces of the riddle to answer it.

What did the baseball glove say to the ball?

__ __ __ __ __ __ __ __ __ __ __ __ !
1 2 3 4 5 6 7 8 9 10 11 12

1. quarterback, racetrak, goalkeeper

   __ __ __ __ __ __ __ __
            1

2. tyebreaker, skydiving, freestyle

   __ __ __ __ __ __ __ __ __
   10   7

3. goalkeeper, horseshoes, wieghtlifting

   __ __ __ __ __ __ __ __ __ __ __ __ __
            5   8

4. infield, scoreboard, backand

   __ __ __ __ __ __ __
   9 4

5. touchdown, owtfeld, shortstop

   __ __ __ __ __ __ __
         3

6. horshoes, homerun, backstroke

   __ __ __ __ __ __ __ __ __
            12   11

7. backboard, playof, quarterback

   __ __ __ __ __ __
   2   6

Swimmer Pairs

FRIENDLY COMPETITION

Name _____

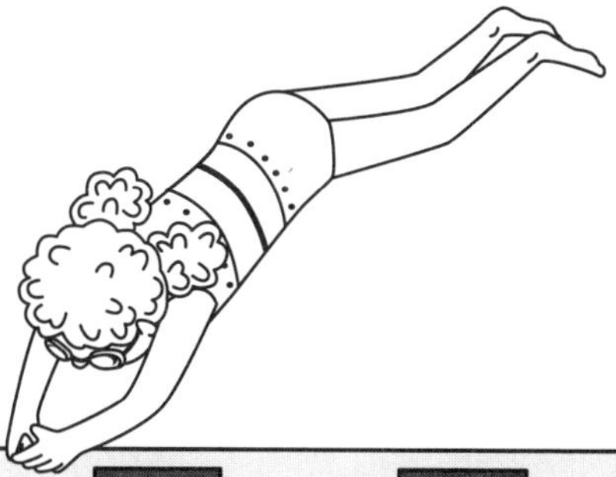

A bunch of words have gone swimming in their own lane. But some words often swim together as a pair. Use these words to make as many compound words as you can. Write them in the box.

1	2	3	4	5	6
down		quarter	off		
	out			goal	breaker
short		back	shoes		
				in	home
hand	sky	style	lifting		
				free	track
horse		board	field		
	race			weight	back
keeper		run	stop		
	stroke			score	diving
tie		play		touch	

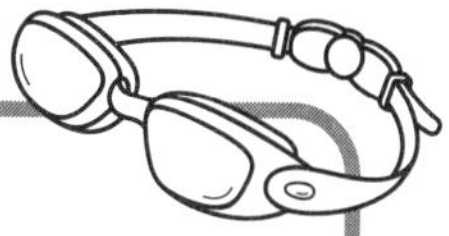

Compound Words

FRIENDLY COMPETITION

Name _____

Competitive Riddles

Read the clue. Write the spelling word to solve the riddle.

| backboard | backhand | freestyle | horseshoes |
| quarterback | racetrack | skydiving | weightlifting |

1. Do this all day long, and you'll soon be strong.   _____
   (ends in a 3-letter suffix)

2. This stroke is the fastest tool to reach the end of the pool.   _____
   (has a silent **e**)

3. I push away anything thrown my way.   _____
   (has consonant and vowel digraphs)

4. On hooves we go "clip-clop"; toss for points and hear us drop.   _____
   (has a hidden **long u** sound)

5. My name ends and starts with two body parts.   _____
   (has the same vowel in both syllables)

6. Fast around me go people and cars, hoping to become stars.   _____
   (ends in a consonant digraph)

7. If you're brave, if you dare, you can do this through the air.   _____
   (has two **long i** sounds)

8. When we play football, I lead them all.   _____
   (has an **r**-controlled vowel)

FRIENDLY COMPETITION

Sporting Chat

Name _____

Emmett and Eun-Ji are texting each other about the baseball game they are watching from different places. Write spelling words to complete the text messages.

> homerun   infield   playoff   scoreboard   shortstop

Can you see the _____?! I can't see if we are winning or not.

The score is tied. Come sit with me! Joy is playing _____, and she's doing great.

I always thought I wasn't a baseball fan, but this is kind of fun. Has she hit a _____ yet?

In the _____ game last year, she hit the ball out of the park. I bet she'll do it again this year!

I see Joy! Look at her taking charge of the _____! I'll come sit with you now.

Athletic Anagrams

FRIENDLY COMPETITION

Name _____

You can change the silly phrases below to spell competiton words.
After you unscramble each phrase, write the spelling word on the line.

> backstroke   goalkeeper   infield   outfield
> racetrack   scoreboard   tiebreaker   touchdown

1. chow donut   _____

2. cork basket   _____

3. crabs rodeo   _____

4. kite bearer   _____

5. car racket   _____

6. fine lid   _____

7. foil duet   _____

8. eagle poker   _____

FRIENDLY COMPETITION

Name _____

Race to the Finish Line!

Students spell words to race around a track.

What You Need

- Word Cards on page 59, cut out
- Game Board on page 60
- die
- a game piece for each player

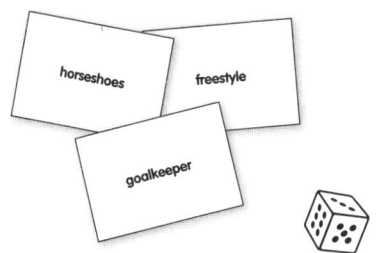

How to Play

The object of the game is to race around the spelling track and reach the finish line first.

1. Put students in groups of four players. Distribute one set of word cards, a game board, and a die to each group and a game piece to each student.

2. Have students choose one person to be the Card Reader. The other three players in the group place their game piece on START. Have students place the cards facedown in a stack.

3. Explain to students that on each player's turn, the Card Reader takes a card from the stack and reads the spelling word aloud. The player spells the word.
   - If the spelling is correct, the player rolls the die and moves the number of spaces shown.
   - If the spelling is incorrect, the player does not move on the board.

4. Continue with each player in turn.

5. Whoever reaches the finish line first wins. That person switches places with the Card Reader to play the game again.

58 FRIENDLY COMPETITION   Spelling Games and Activities • EMC 8275 • © Evan-Moor Corporation

FRIENDLY COMPETITION
Word Cards

horseshoes	skydiving	weightlifting
backstroke	freestyle	backhand
racetrack	infield	outfield
backboard	shortstop	goalkeeper
quarterback	touchdown	homerun
playoff	tiebreaker	scoreboard

FRIENDLY COMPETITION
Game Board

Name _____

LET'S GO OUT TO EAT!

Practice spelling and using these words about where people dine and what they eat.

- ☐ restaurant
- ☐ socialize
- ☐ cashier
- ☐ cafeteria
- ☐ appetizer
- ☐ delicious
- ☐ delicatessen
- ☐ beverage
- ☐ cuisine
- ☐ buffet
- ☐ condiment
- ☐ vegetarian
- ☐ gourmet
- ☐ utensils
- ☐ international
- ☐ receipt
- ☐ chopsticks
- ☐ cultural

SPELLING TIPS

☆ Try dividing long words into syllables and then spell each syllable: **national**: **na|tion|al**.

☆ **R-controlled** vowels are any vowel followed by an **r**. The **r** changes the sound of the vowel. They sound different from long and short vowels. Examples: **farm, water, turkey**

☆ Some English words come from the French language. They keep the French pronunciation and have a silent **t** at the end: **filet**.

LET'S GO OUT TO EAT! 61

LET'S GO OUT TO EAT!

Hidden Meal

What's on your plate today? Read the word in each space.
Color each space following these rules:

- Use brown for words that have 5 syllables.
- Use black for words that have a silent letter.
- Use blue for words that have 3 syllables.
- Use red for words that have a consonant digraph.
- Use green for all other words.

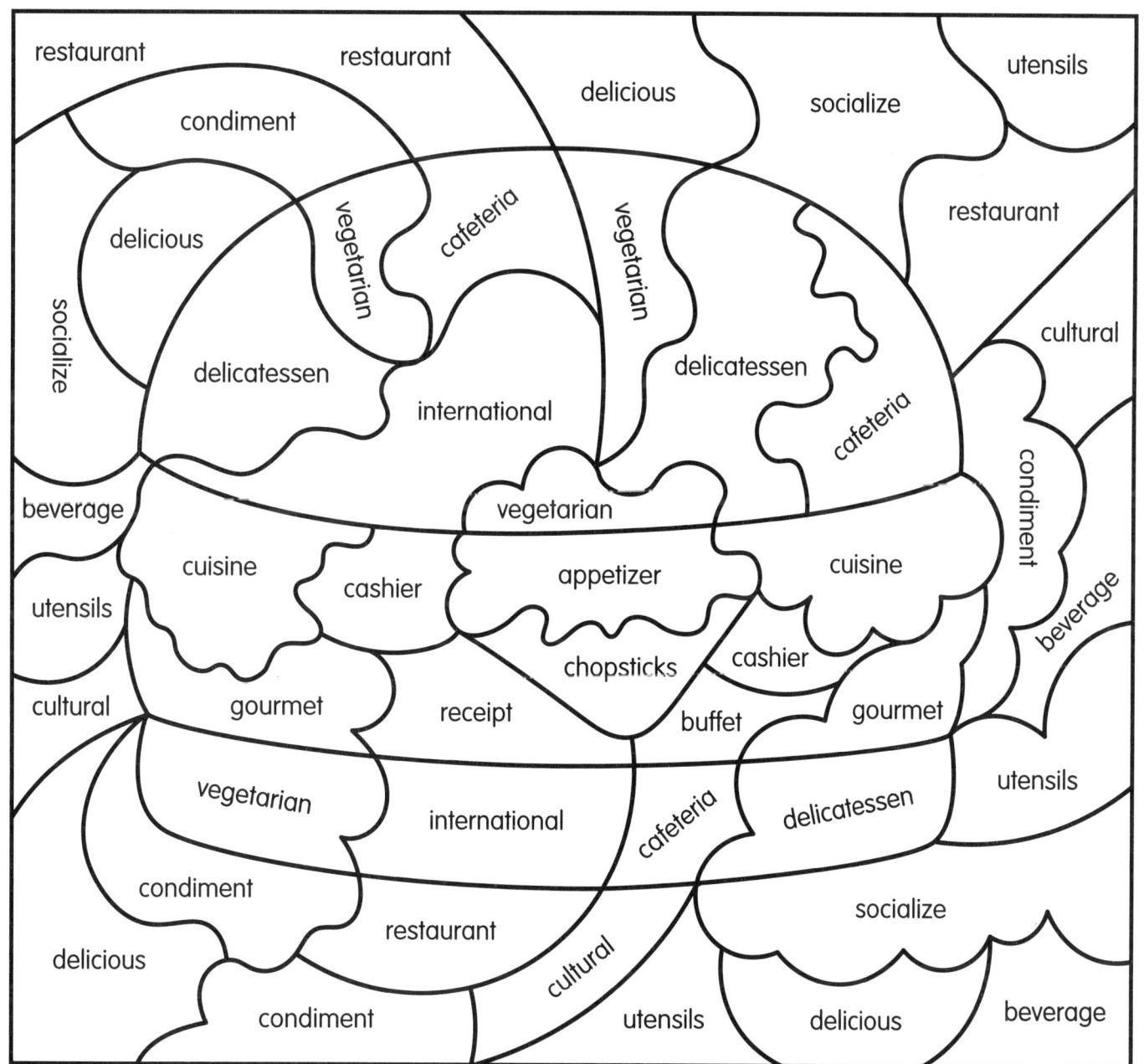

LET'S GO OUT TO EAT!

Name _____

Mixed-up Menu

Oliver went to a new restaurant. The menu is full of scrambled words! Oliver underlined them. Write them correctly below.

> appetizer   beverage   condiments   delicious
> gourmet   restaurant   vegetarian

WELCOME TO BON APPETIT SUTRRANETA

Choose an

PPEAZTREI
Caesar salad
Cheese plate
Soup of the day

Try our

BURGERS
Beef
Chicken

with unlimited cmosnedint

Try our

PIZZAS
Margherita
Pepperoni
Eeaviangrt

Choose a

EVGBAREE
Sparkling soda
Mineral water
Coffee

Choose a

EUOTRGM DESSERT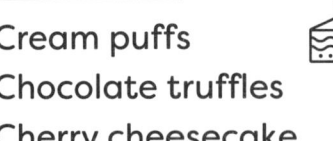
Cream puffs
Chocolate truffles
Cherry cheesecake

We serve eludocsii food, made with

_____   _____   _____

_____   _____   _____

LET'S GO OUT TO EAT!

Let's Do Takeout!

See how many words you can take out of each container. Look at the letters in each spelling word. Use them to make other words. Write them on each takeout container.

cultural

cart cat curl cut
rut rat tall ultra

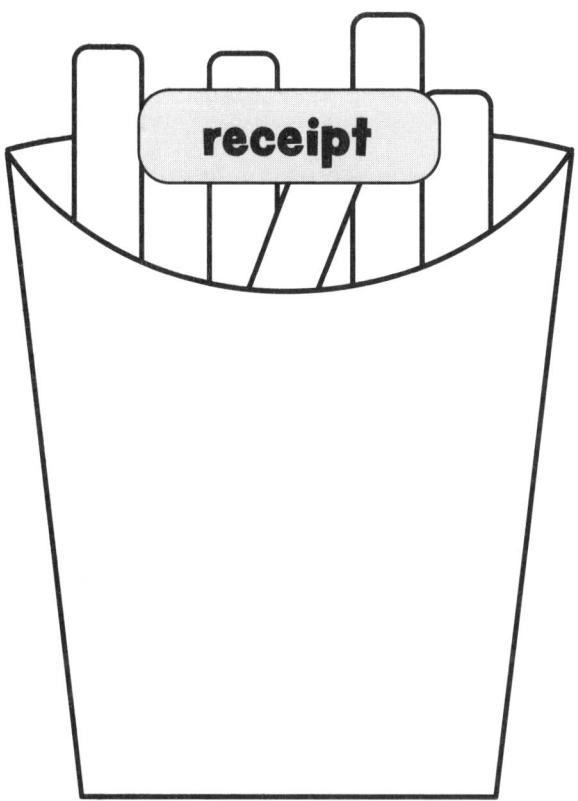

receipt

beverage

condiment

socialize

A Neighborhood Stroll

LET'S GO OUT TO EAT!

Name _____

Carlos is strolling past stores in his town. Some of the places he sees have misspelled signs! Circle any misspelled words. Write them correctly below.

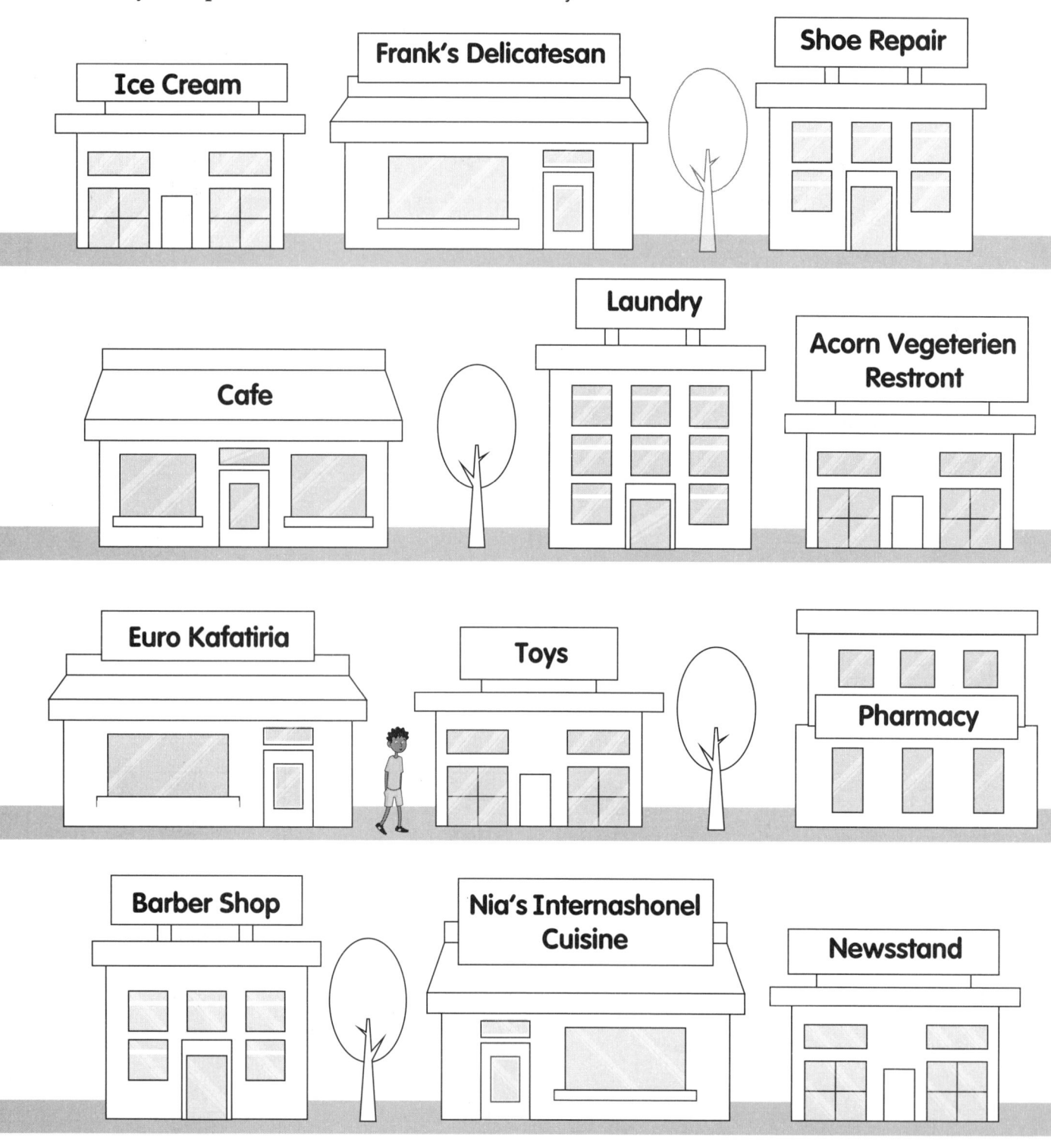

_____ _____ _____

_____ _____ _____

LET'S GO OUT TO EAT!

LET'S GO OUT TO EAT!

Secret Dishes

Name _____

Look closely at the starting, ending, and vowel sounds of the clue words in the example. They describe a dining word in the box. The dining word will have the same sounds, but the spelling may be different from the clue words.

| buffet | cashier | condiment | cuisine |
| cultural | receipt | restaurant | utensils |

Example

| starts like **bagel** | ends like **may** |
| vowel sounds like **weigh** | same syllables as **provide** |

Center: **buffet**

| starts like **reward** | ends like **soft** |
| vowel sounds like **bean** | same syllables as **remind** |

| starts like **castle** | ends like **lane** |
| vowel sounds like **tree** | same syllables as **remove** |

| starts like **unicorn** | ends like **cars** |
| vowel sounds like **pet** | same syllables as **banana** |

66 LET'S GO OUT TO EAT! Spelling Games and Activities • EMC 8275 • © Evan-Moor Corporation

LET'S GO OUT TO EAT!

Food Tour

Name _____

Fatima is making a poster about her family's trip to Southeast Asia. The vowels fell off of her poster! Finish the words using the vowels in the box. Cross off each vowel after you use it.

a	a	a	a	e	e	e
e	e	e	i	i	i	i
i	i	i	i	i	o	o
o	o	o	u	u	u	u

This is me using ch__pst__cks for the first time! I'm eating a d__l__c__ __ __s noodle bowl in Hanoi.

This is the night market in Siem Reap! I made friends with the c__sh__ __r at one of the shops. It was nice to s__c__ __l__ze with new people.

We went to a g__ __rm__t b__ff__t in Bangkok. I ate so much!

Malaysian c__ __s__n__ was tasty. I had so much fun on my first int__rn__t__ __n__l trip!

LET'S GO OUT TO EAT! 67

LET'S GO OUT TO EAT!

Would You Rather...

Name _____

Students talk and write in pairs as they answer "Would You Rather" questions and write spelling words.

What You Need

- Would You Rather on page 69
- Our Spelling Words on page 70
- 2 dice
- pencil

What You Do

1. Put students in pairs. Distribute a copy of Would You Rather and Our Spelling Words to each pair, along with the dice. Have each student write his or her name at the top of one column on the Our Spelling Words sheet.

2. Explain to students that they will take turns choosing between two options. To start, Player 1 rolls the pair of dice and adds the total number rolled. Player 2 finds that number on the Would You Rather sheet and reads the two options on that row to Player 1. Player 1 chooses an option. Player 2 then tells Player 1 the underlined spelling word in the chosen option.

3. Player 1 writes the spelling word under his or her name on the Our Spelling Words sheet. Player 2 checks the spelling. If it is correct, it is now Player 2's turn. If the spelling is incorrect, Player 2 can offer tips on how to spell the word.

4. Continue until each player has 6 words spelled correctly on the sheet.

LET'S GO OUT TO EAT!

Would You Rather

If you roll...	Would you rather...		
2	eat all your food without any **utensils**?	or	eat all of your food using only **chopsticks**?
3	never order an **appetizer** when eating out?	or	never order a **beverage** when eating out?
4	go to a **cultural** food festival with all your friends?	or	go to a **vegetarian** potluck with all your friends?
5	eat at a **restaurant** every night for the rest of your life?	or	eat a **delicious** homemade meal every night for the rest of your life?
6	try a dessert from every **cuisine** in the world?	or	try every kind of **condiment** in the world?
7	work as a sandwich maker at a **delicatessen**?	or	work as a **cashier** at a health food store?
8	eat a **gourmet** meal at a fancy restaurant?	or	eat whatever you want at an all-you-can-eat **buffet**?
9	eat a meal and **socialize** with friends at your house?	or	try a new kind of food alone at a **cafeteria**?
10	keep a **receipt** for every meal you eat from around the world?	or	keep a photograph of every **delicious** meal you eat?
11	go on an **international** street-food tour?	or	go on a state-wide **gourmet**-food tour?
12	eat at a new **restaurant** every day for the rest of your life?	or	eat at your favorite **delicatessen** every day for the rest of your life?

© Evan-Moor Corporation • EMC 8275 • Spelling Games and Activities

LET'S GO OUT TO EAT!

LET'S GO OUT TO EAT!

Our Spelling Words

Name: _____   Name: _____

1. _____   1. _____

2. _____   2. _____

3. _____   3. _____

4. _____   4. _____

5. _____   5. _____

6. _____   6. _____

Name _____

HELPING OTHERS

Practice spelling and using these words about collecting money to help others in need.

- ☐ volunteer
- ☐ charity
- ☐ contribute
- ☐ fundraiser
- ☐ finance
- ☐ campaign
- ☐ organizer
- ☐ assistance
- ☐ marathon
- ☐ donation
- ☐ relief
- ☐ pledge
- ☐ collection
- ☐ rescue
- ☐ auction
- ☐ community
- ☐ nonprofit
- ☐ benefit

SPELLING TIPS

⭐ If a **c** comes before an **i**, **y**, or **e**, it is soft and sounds like **s**: **race**.
   If a **c** comes before a different letter, it is hard and sounds like **k**: **care**.

⭐ Words ending in the **nce** sound in **convince** are almost always spelled with a **c**, not an **s**.

⭐ Most multisyllable words have a **schwa** sound. The schwa sound is found in unaccented syllables. There is no rule for which vowel to use to spell it.

⭐ Vowel digraphs are two vowels that have one sound. Examples include **ee**, **ai**, **ie**, **ue**, and **au**: **feed**, **mail**, **believe**, **value**, **cause**.

© Evan-Moor Corporation • EMC 8275 • Spelling Games and Activities

HELPING OTHERS 71

HELPING OTHERS

Marathon of Hope

Name _____

Kirk is running in a marathon to raise money for cancer research. The marathon's route has words with a **hard c** sound and words with a vowel digraph. Draw a line to show the marathon path that Kirk is following.

HELPING OTHERS
Schwa Helpers

Name _____

Schwa sounds are the quiet helpers in a word. Most words with more than one syllable have a schwa sound. Read each word in the box and decide which vowels are making each schwa sound. Circle the vowels. Then write each word in its Schwa Zone. If a word has more than one schwa, write the word in each zone. Use a different color for each zone

| assistance | collection | community | contribute |
| mar(a)thon | nonprofit | organizer | relief |

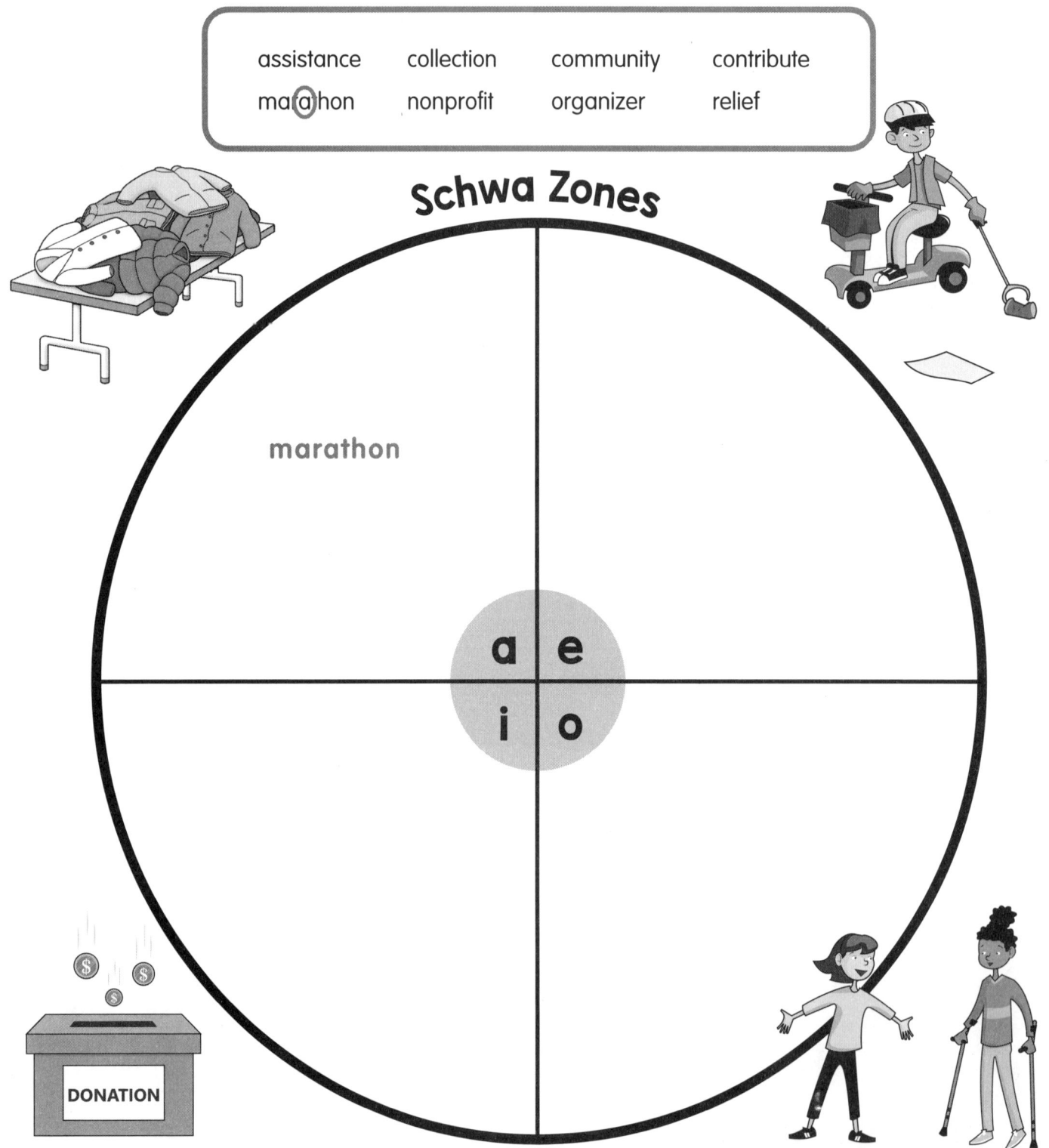

Schwa Zones

marathon

a | e
i | o

HELPING OTHERS

Call for Support

A local shelter for unhoused people is looking for support. Write the words from the box to complete the poster.

> charity   collection   community
> donations   nonprofit   volunteers

We're looking for _____!

Support our shelter for unhoused people and lend a hand to people in need.

You can make the difference in your _____ today!

Ways to help:
- cooking meals
- gathering cash _____
- the _____ of clothes for those in need

Join us for this _____ event!

📅 November 23, 2023
9:00 a.m.–5:00 p.m.

📍 12389 Light Street
Aurora, CO 80020

We are a _____ organization.
Please visit our website for more details.

HELPING OTHERS

Asking for Help

Name _____

Levi is sending an e-mail to family and friends to collect money to help others in need. Some of the letters are missing. Finish the words using the letters in the box. Cross off each letter after you use it.

```
a  a  c  c  c  d  d  e  e  e  e  e  e
g  i  m  m  n  n  n  n  o  o  u  u  u
```

New Message

To Friends and Family

Subject Can you help with earthquake rel ___ ___ f?

Hi everyone!

I'm looking for some assist ___ ___ ___ ___. There was a huge earthquake overseas last week. Res ___ ___ ___ teams are helping.

I want to help out and c ___ ___ tribute in my own way!

My mom said I can ask my c ___ ___ ___ ___ nity for help. I decided to host a fu ___ ___ raiser with my friends. We want to help you with your chores!

- Do you need someone to mow your lawn? I can help you with that!
- Do you need someone to rake your leaves? Roman can help you with that!
- Do you need someone to wash your car? Ebony can help you with that!

Just ple ___ ___ ___ money for each chore. Every penny will b ___ ___ ___ fit the people in the earthquake. My school is also having an ___ ___ ___ tion to raise money next Thursday. I hope you can help!

Levi

HELPING OTHERS

Name _____

Brainstorming Together

Arjun and his classmates are brainstorming what they can do to raise money for others at their school. Read each idea. Circle any misspelled words. Write them correctly below.

Arjun

I think we should compagn for animal rights. There is a local cherite that needs help.

_____ _____

Hannah

Maybe we could host a school merithon? We can ask people to plege money for each mile that students run.

_____ _____

Lulu

I like these ideas! I also want to do a fundrazer to help with tornado relief. We could help finanse resque efforts.

_____ _____

_____

Anagram Aid

HELPING OTHERS

Name _____

You can change the silly phrases below to spell helpful words. After you unscramble each phrase, write the spelling word on the line.

> auction   benefit   campaign   donation
> finance   marathon   organizer   volunteer

1. nap magic _____

2. I toucan _____

3. true novel _____

4. tad onion _____

5. tin beef _____

6. zero grain _____

7. face inn _____

8. roman hat _____

HELPING OTHERS

Name _____

Spelling Bee Fundraiser

Students play in groups of four and "raise" money for a cause.

What You Need

- Word Cards on page 79, cut out
- Play Money on page 80, cut out

How to Play

The object of the game is to spell the most words correctly and raise money for a group that the class cares about.

1. Put students in groups of four players. Distribute a set of word cards and $180 in play money to each group. Have students place the word cards facedown in a stack and the play money in another stack.

2. Have students choose one player in each group to start as the Reader. The group decides on a cause to support in their Spelling Bee Fundraiser. Suggestions:
   - animal rights
   - environment cleanup
   - helping recent refugees
   - emergency relief, such as flood rescue
   - research to cure a disease

3. The Reader takes the top word card and reads the word aloud. A player who knows how to spell the word shouts, "I'll spell It!" The player then spells the word aloud.
   - If the spelling is correct, the Reader gives the player $10.
   - If the spelling is incorrect, the Reader tells the player and then repeats the word to give another player a chance to spell it.

4. Continue until the group has correctly spelled 6 words. All group members count their money. Whoever raised the most money is the next Reader.

5. Continue until there are no more word cards left or a time limit has been reached.

6. Have each group report the total amount it raised. Add them all up to see how much the class made.

HELPING OTHERS

Word Cards

volunteer	charity	contribute
fundraiser	finance	campaign
organizer	assistance	marathon
donation	relief	pledge
collection	rescue	auction
community	nonprofit	benefit

HELPING OTHERS

Play Money

Name _____

WILDLIFE

Practice spelling and using these words about animals in the wild, where they live, and what they face.

- ☐ gorilla
- ☐ leopard
- ☐ cheetah
- ☐ rhinoceros
- ☐ hippopotamus
- ☐ wilderness
- ☐ sanctuary
- ☐ ecosystem
- ☐ savanna
- ☐ safari
- ☐ conservation
- ☐ endangered
- ☐ species
- ☐ threatened
- ☐ extinct
- ☐ biodiversity
- ☐ predator
- ☐ ferocious

SPELLING TIPS

⭐ **R-controlled** vowels are any vowel followed by an **r**. The **r** changes the sound of the vowel. They sound different from long and short vowels. Examples: tig**er**, sh**ark**, **or**ca

⭐ Vowel digraphs are two vowels that have one sound. Examples include **ee**, **ea**, **ou**, **ie**, and **eo**: g**ee**se, l**ea**f, r**ou**gh, f**ie**ld, l**eo**pard.

⭐ If a **c** comes before an **i**, **y**, or **e**, it is soft and sounds like **s**: **s**pace.

Sometimes **ci** followed by other vowels sounds like **sh**: **sp**a**ci**ous.

If a **c** comes before a different letter, it is hard and sounds like **k**: **c**obra.

WILDLIFE 81

WILDLIFE
Safari Search

Name _____

Elana is on a safari with her friend. Look at the safari map. They will watch animals in every place with a word that includes an **r**-controlled vowel. Draw a line from the jeep to each place they will go on the way to their cabin at the end.

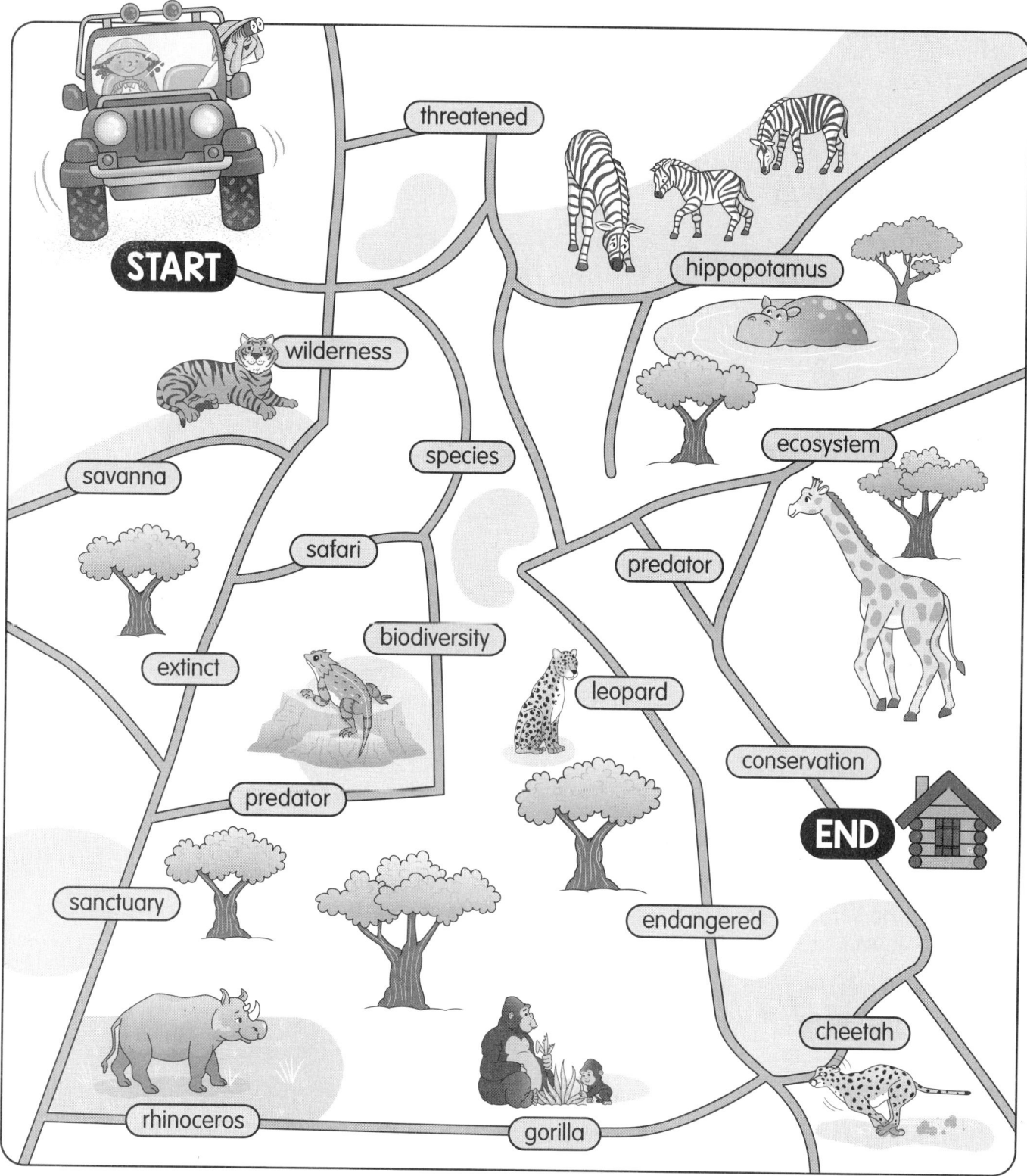

WILDLIFE

Hidden in the Wild

Name _____

Look closely at the starting, ending, and vowel sounds of the clue words in the example. They describe a wildlife word in the box. The wildlife word will have the same sounds, but the spelling may be different from the clue words.

| ecosystem | extinct | safari |
| sanctuary | savanna | threatened |

Example

starts like **think**	ends like **find**
threatened	
vowel sounds like **sweat**	same syllables as **button**

starts like **safety**	ends like **tree**
vowel sounds like **car**	same syllables as **computer**

starts like **even**	ends like **beam**
vowel sounds like **cream**	same syllables as **territory**

starts like **sweet**	ends like **ability**
vowel sounds like **ankle**	same syllables as **caterpillar**

© Evan-Moor Corporation • EMC 8275 • Spelling Games and Activities

WILDLIFE 83

WILDLIFE

Spy the Species

What's hiding in the forest? Read the word in each space.
Color each space following these rules.

- Use black for words with the **ea**, **ou**, or **eo** vowel digraph.
- Use white for words that end in the vowel **a** or **i**.
- Use brown for words with a **soft c** sound.
- Use blue for words with a **hard c** sound.
- Use green for all other words.

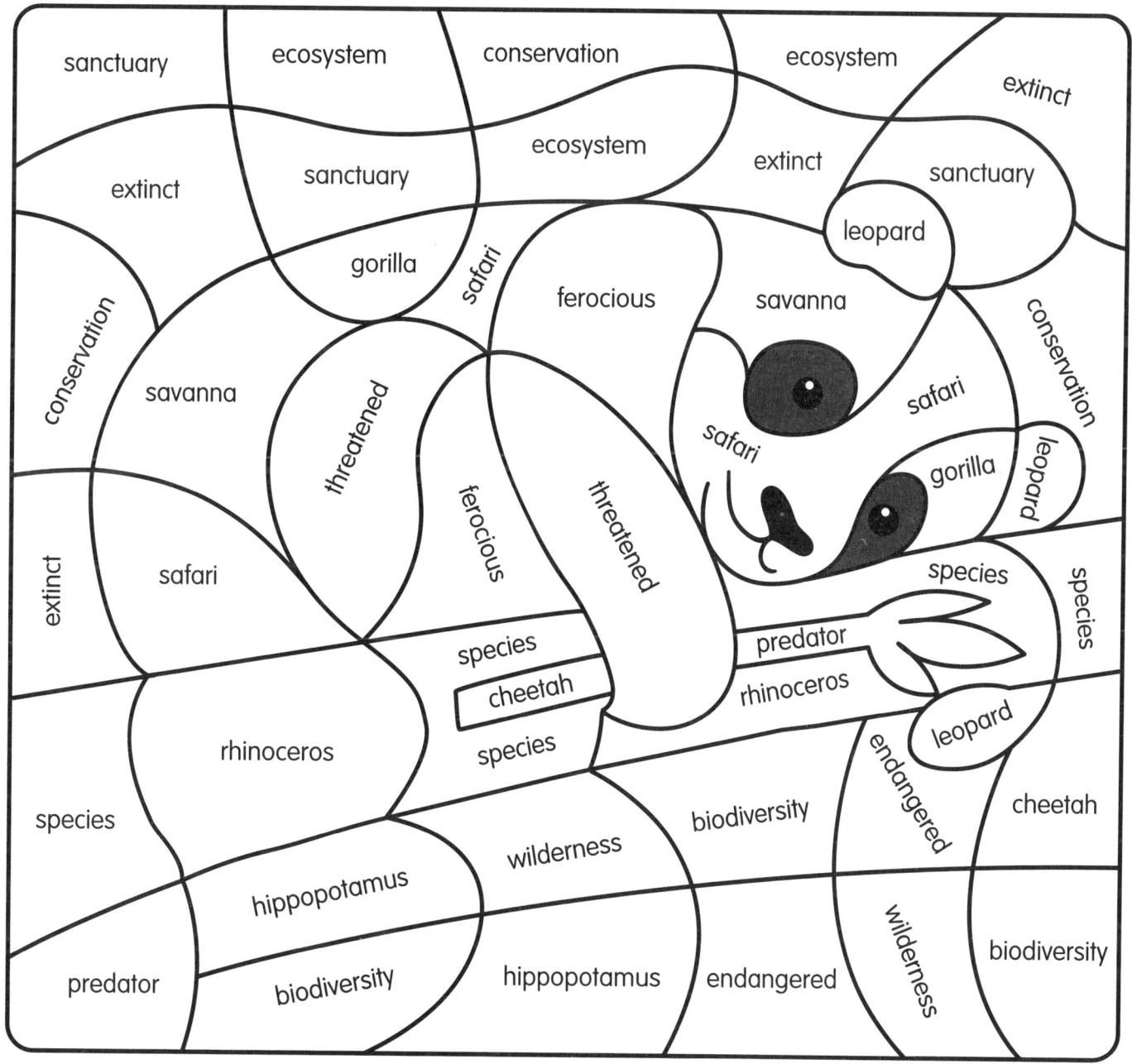

WILDLIFE

Exploring the Wild

Name _____

You never know what you will find in the wild!
Look at the letters in each spelling word.
Use them to make other words.
Write them on each animal.

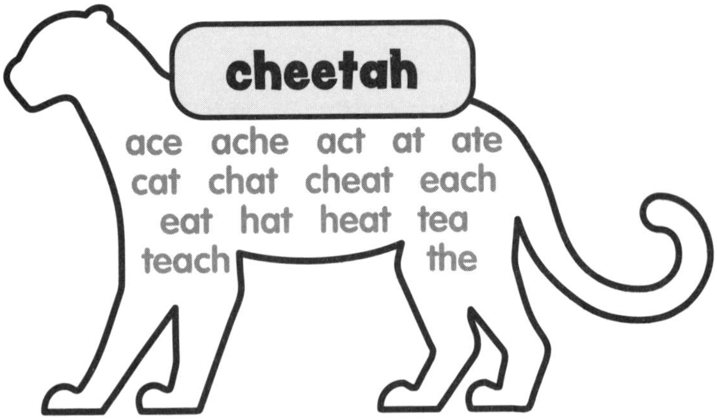

cheetah

ace ache act at ate
cat chat cheat each
eat hat heat tea
teach   the

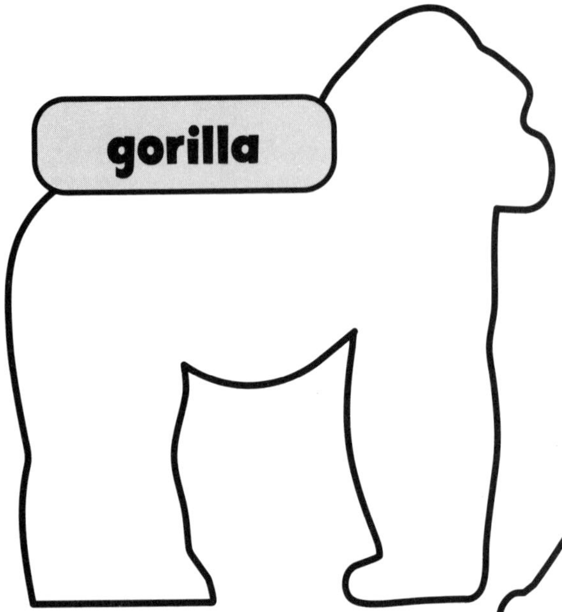

gorilla

hippopotamus

rhinoceros

leopard

© Evan-Moor Corporation • EMC 8275 • Spelling Games and Activities

WILDLIFE 85

WILDLIFE

Pluck the Vowels

Name _____

The vowels fell out of the words below! Luckily, the toucan has pulled off some vowels growing in the forest.

Finish the words using the vowels in the box. Cross off each vowel after you use it.

```
a  a  a  a  a  a  e  e
e  e  e  e  e  e  e  e
e  e  e  i  i  i  i  o
o  o  o  u  u
```

1. bi ___ d ___ v ___ rs ___ ty

2. pr ___ d ___ t ___ r

3. w ___ ld ___ rn ___ ss

4. ___ nd ___ ng ___ r ___ d

5. f ___ r ___ c ___ ___ ___ s

6. thr ___ ___ t ___ n ___ d

7. ch ___ ___ t ___ h

8. s ___ nct ___ ___ ry

86 WILDLIFE Spelling Games and Activities • EMC 8275 • © Evan-Moor Corporation

(WILDLIFE)

Sneaky Riddles

Name _____

One word in each group is spelled incorrectly. Find the word and spell it correctly in the spaces below the group. Then write the numbered letters in the matching spaces of the riddle to answer it.

What kind of jungle cat doesn't play fair?

___ ___ ___ ___ ___ ___ ___ ___ !
 1   2   3   4   5   6   7   8

1. threatened, gorilla, indangared

   ___ ___ ___ ___ ___ ___ ___ ___ ___ ___
                  7

2. biodevercity, hippopotamus, rhinoceros

   ___ ___ ___ ___ ___ ___ ___ ___ ___ ___ ___ ___
                        5

3. consarvation, sanctuary, wilderness

   ___ ___ ___ ___ ___ ___ ___ ___ ___ ___ ___ ___
        2

4. savanna, prediter, species

   ___ ___ ___ ___ ___ ___ ___ ___
                1

5. ecosystem, gorilla, hipopotamis

   ___ ___ ___ ___ ___ ___ ___ ___ ___ ___ ___ ___
    8   6

6. leopard, sanctwoary, ferocious

   ___ ___ ___ ___ ___ ___ ___ ___ ___
                       7

7. rinoceros, safari, extinct

   ___ ___ ___ ___ ___ ___ ___ ___ ___
        3   4

WILDLIFE
Safari Spelling

Name _____

Students spell words together on a safari tour!

What You Need
- Spelling List and Safari Die on page 89
- Safari Game Board on page 90
- game pieces
- scissors
- glue or tape
- paper
- pencil

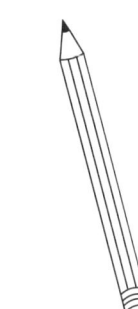
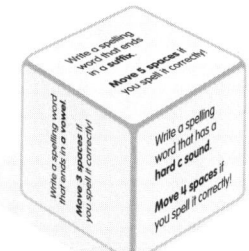

How to Play

The object of the game is to move through the safari as quickly as possible.

1. Put students in pairs. Distribute a game board and a Spelling List and Safari Die sheet to each pair. Make sure they have scissors, glue or tape, a blank sheet of paper, and a pencil. Each student should have a game piece.

2. Have students cut out the spelling list and the die. Have them make the die by folding on the lines to make a cube and gluing or taping the tabs. Then have them place their game pieces on the START space on the game board.

3. Explain to students that Player 1 rolls the safari die and reads the top side aloud. Player 2 then finds a word on the Spelling List that fits the description and reads it for Player 1 to write on the paper. Player 2 checks the spelling.

   - If the spelling is correct, Player 1 moves his or her game piece as shown on the die.

   - If the spelling is incorrect, Player 2 can give tips on how to spell the word. Player 1 gets one more try to spell the word.

4. Players switch roles each turn until both reach the END space on the game board.

5. Players say "Safari complete!" The teacher then checks the spelling words.

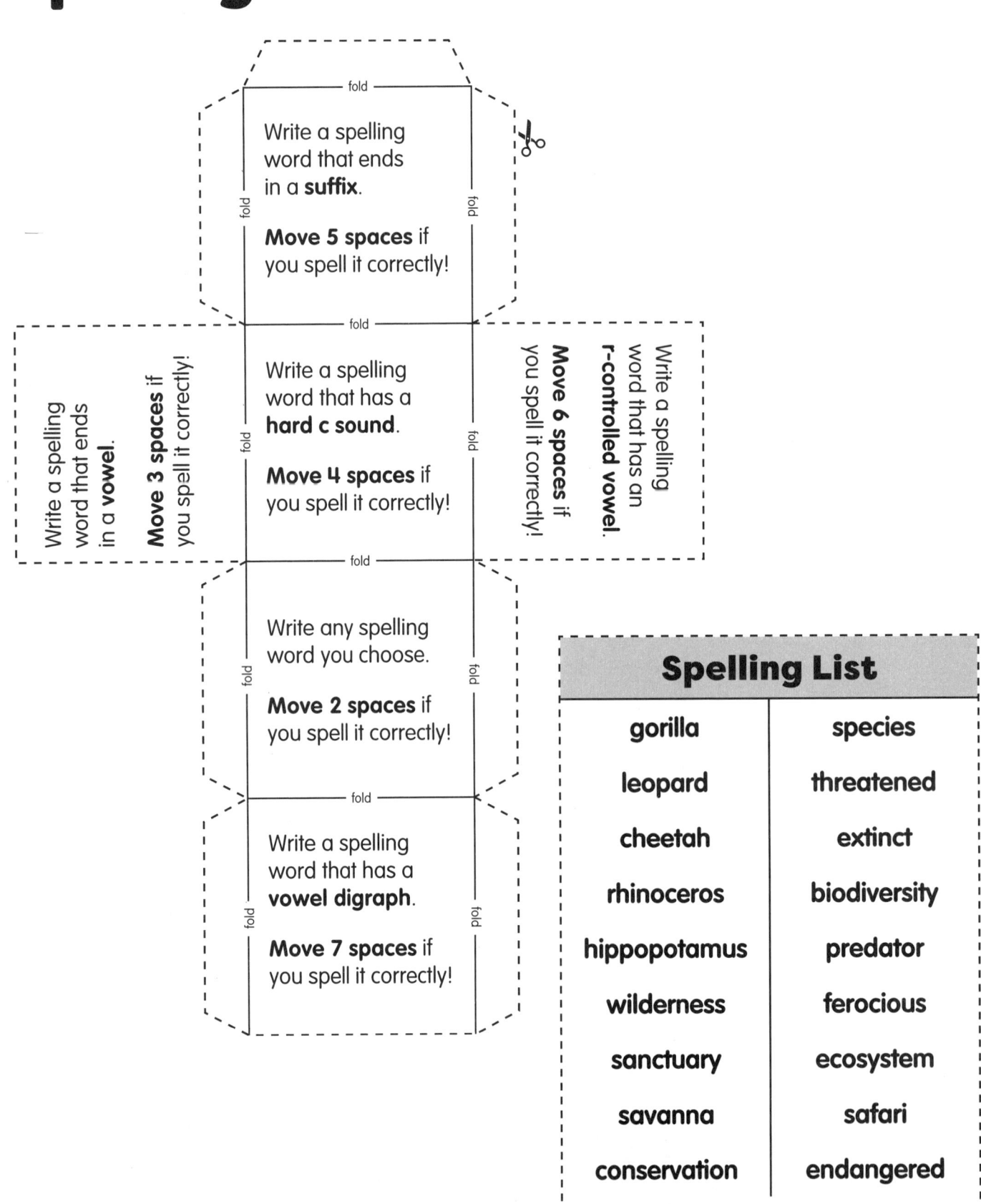

WILDLIFE
Safari Game Board

Extra Practice Worksheets

This section provides an additional 525 words to give students even more practice with spelling patterns and word study! The activity pages can be used independently or to enhance *Building Spelling Skills* weekly lessons.

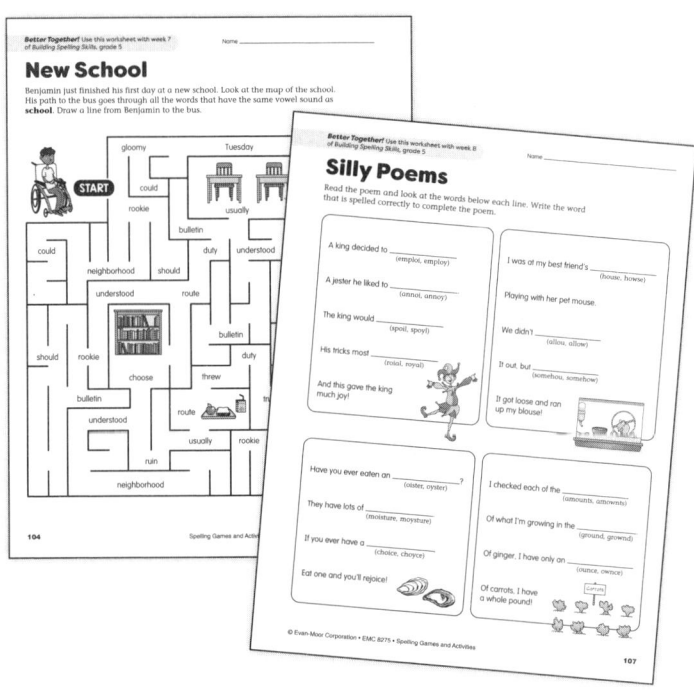

Better Together!

The worksheets in this section correspond to each week in *Building Spelling Skills*, grade 5.

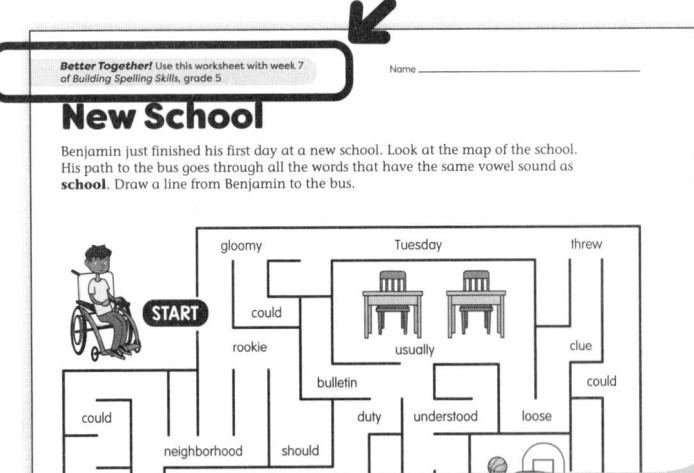

Better Together! Use this worksheet with week 1 of *Building Spelling Skills*, grade 5

Name _____

A "Beary" Silly Riddle

Unscramble each word. Then write the numbered letters in the matching spaces of the riddle to answer it.

another	began	city	grudge	once
rough	thumb	trouble	umpire	very

What do you call a bear with no teeth?

___ ___ ___ ___ ___ ___   ___ ___ ___ ___ !
 1   2   3   4   5   6   7   8   9   10

1. orghu

   ___ ___ ___ ___ ___
         2

2. udregg

   ___ ___ ___ ___ ___ ___
         3

3. humtb

   ___ ___ ___ ___ ___
            4

4. ncoe

   ___ ___ ___ ___
         8

5. eaothrn

   ___ ___ ___ ___ ___ ___ ___
   1

6. rebtluo

   ___ ___ ___ ___ ___ ___ ___
               7

7. anbge

   ___ ___ ___ ___ ___
               9

8. evyr

   ___ ___ ___ ___
            10

9. mrepui

   ___ ___ ___ ___ ___ ___
         5

10. tciy

    ___ ___ ___ ___
               6

Better Together! Use this worksheet with week 1 of *Building Spelling Skills*, grade 5

Name _____

Look More Closely!

Look at the letters in each spelling word.
Use them to make other words.
Write them on each magnifying glass.

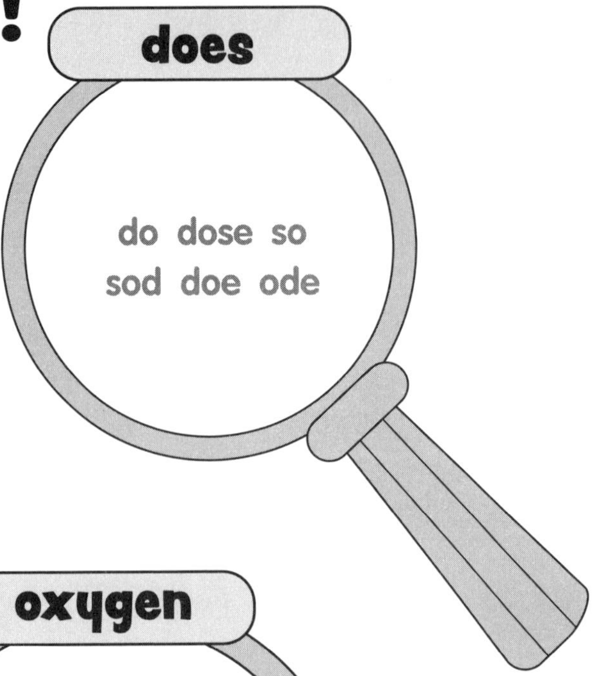

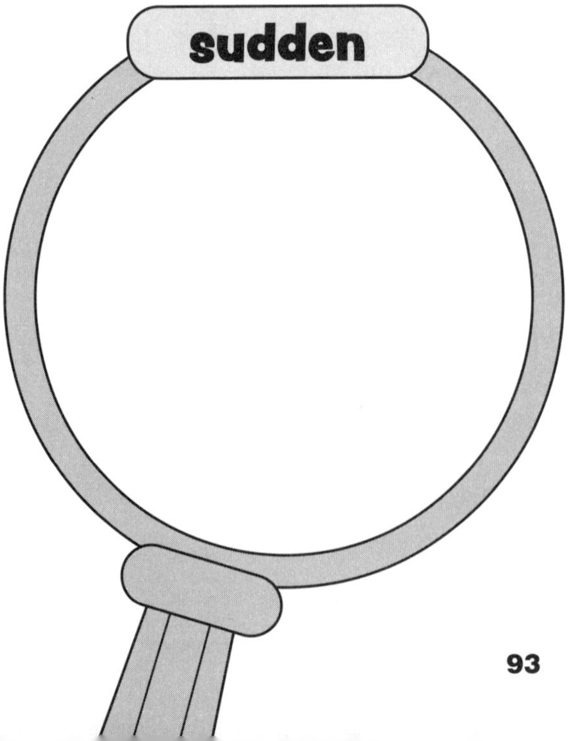

does

do dose so
sod doe ode

cousin

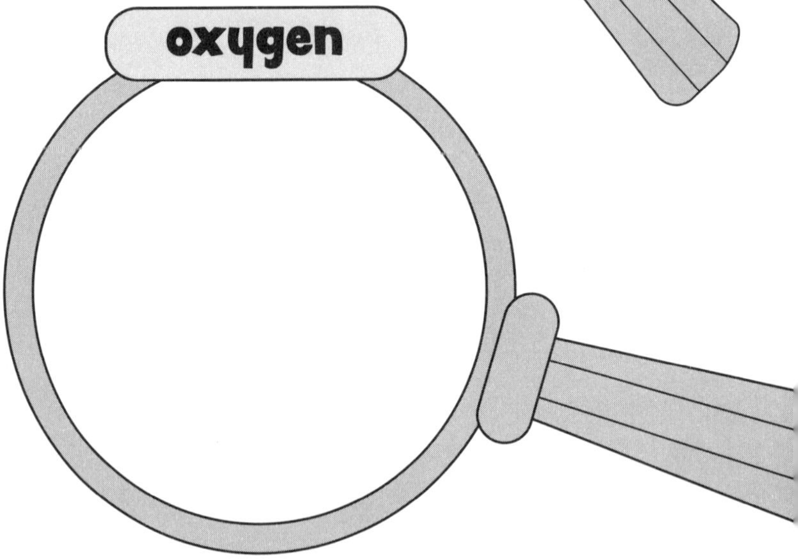

oxygen

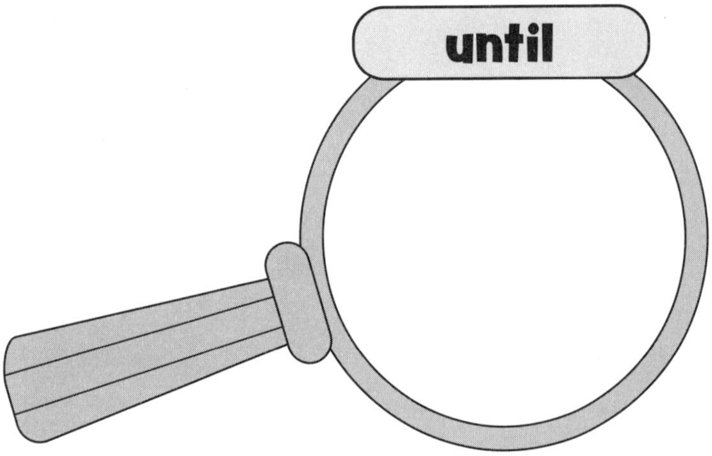

sudden

until

Better Together! Use this worksheet with week 2 of *Building Spelling Skills*, grade 5

Follow the Vowel Teams

Nicolas is going to Olivia's house to play cards. Look at the map of the city bus stops. The bus he takes goes on every street with a name that has a vowel digraph with a **long a** sound. Draw a line from Nicolas to each stop his bus will make.

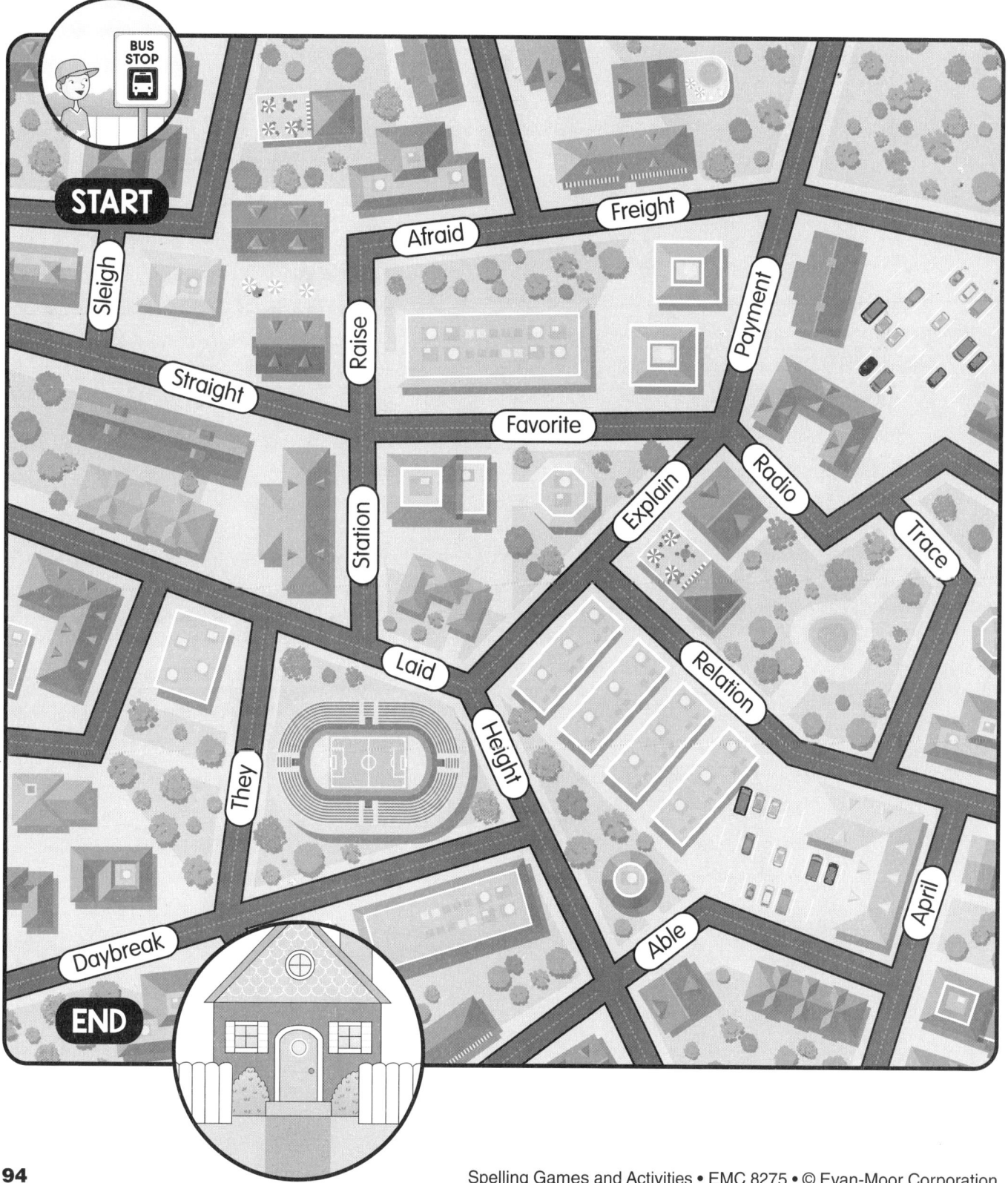

Vowel Weather

The words below are missing their vowels! Luckily, there are vowels falling from the sky. Finish the words using the vowels in the cloud. Cross off each vowel after you use it.

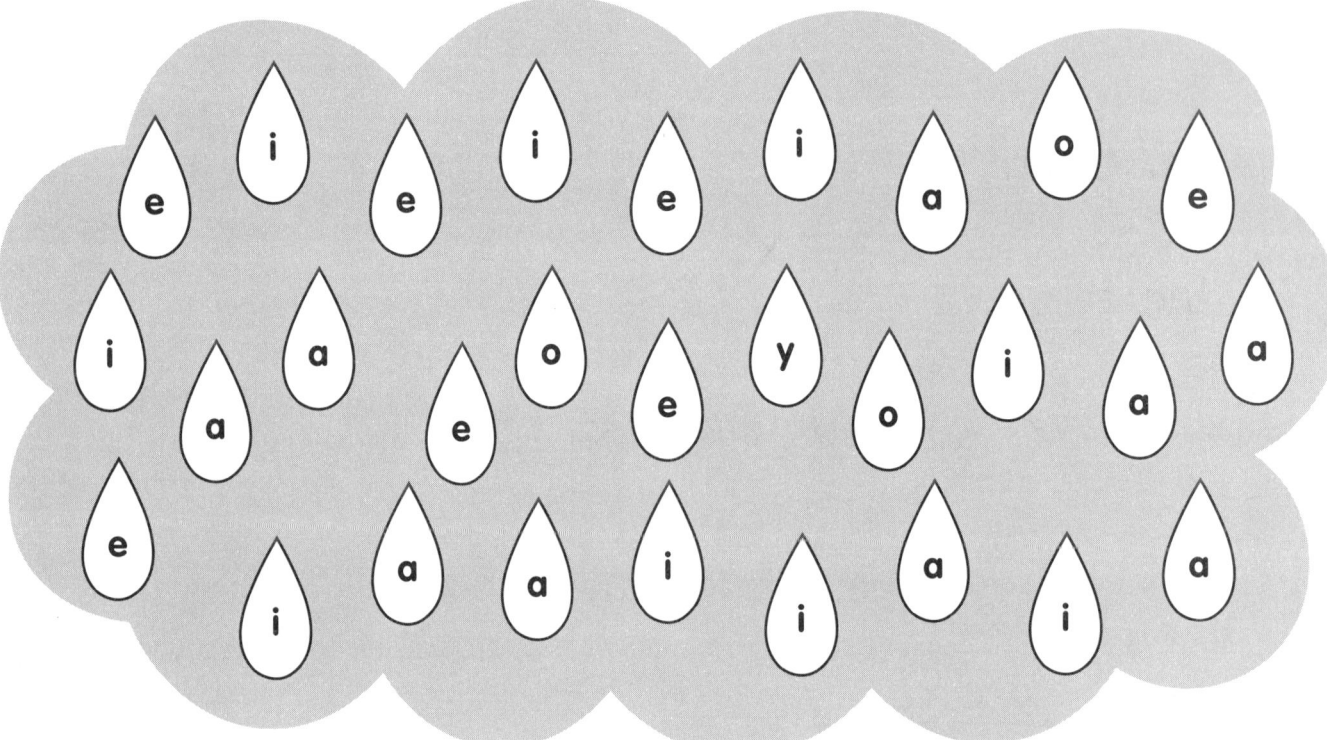

1. l_____d

2. sl_____gh

3. r_____s___

4. ___xpl_____n

5. str_____ght

6. fr_____ght

7. f___v___r___t___

8. r___l___t_____n

9. r___d_____

10. d_____br_____k

Better Together! Use this worksheet with week 3 of *Building Spelling Skills*, grade 5

Name _____

Dear Aunt Iti

Meera wrote to her Aunt Iti. Read her e-mail. Some letters are missing. Finish the words using the letters in the box. Cross off each letter after you use it.

```
a  a  a  a  e  e  e  e  e  e  e
e  e  e  e  u  u  u  u  u  y  y
```

New message

To: Aunt Iti
Subject: Hello, hello!

How have you b____ ____n? You visited us onl____ two months ago, but I miss you!

I've had a great summer, but I feel read____ for school now. I am going to join the chess club. Mom said it was an un____s____al choice because I'm always running around.

Did you know my sister's birthday is next week? She turns fift____ ____n! Mom said she can take driving lessons, even though car f____ ____l is so expensive. If she gets a car, she can ____ ____sily drive me to soccer practice. I made a good kick in my last game. The other coach thought it was out of bounds, but the refer____ ____ said it was inside. It helped us score a goal!

Have you made fut____r____ plans to visit us again? Pl____ ____se let us know as soon as you do. We're all ____ ____ger to have you come here again.

As Mom would say, I hope you're having a b____ ____ ____tiful week!

Meera

Better Together! Use this worksheet with week 3 of *Building Spelling Skills*, grade 5

Name _____

Use Your Clues

Look closely at the starting, ending, and vowel sounds of the clue words in the example. They describe a mystery word in the box. The mystery word will have the same sounds, but the spelling may be different from the clue words. Write the mystery word.

> communicate   cube   cute   easily
> ecology   maybe   universe   unusual

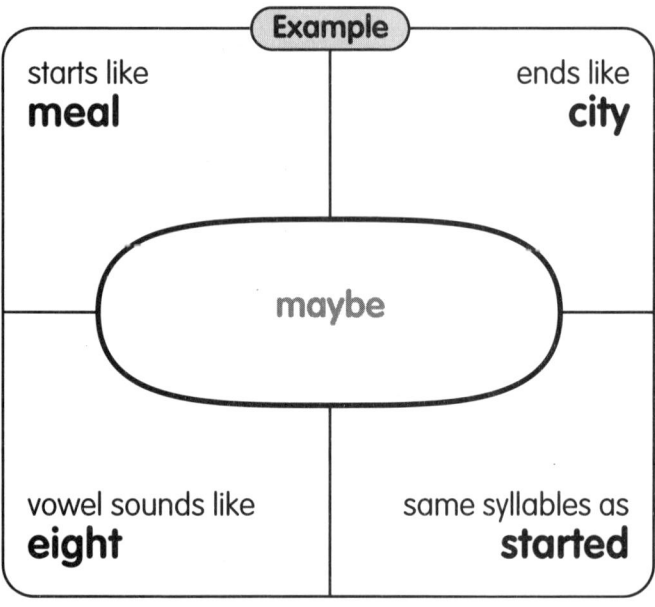

Example

starts like **meal** | ends like **city**
maybe
vowel sounds like **eight** | same syllables as **started**

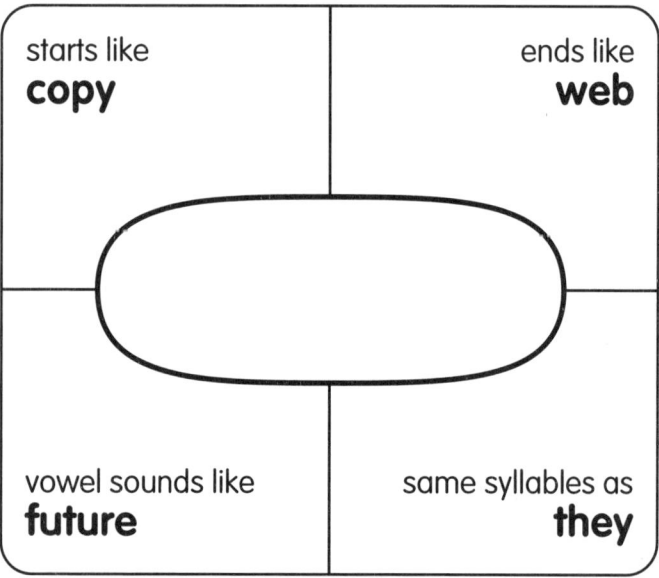

starts like **copy** | ends like **web**
vowel sounds like **future** | same syllables as **they**

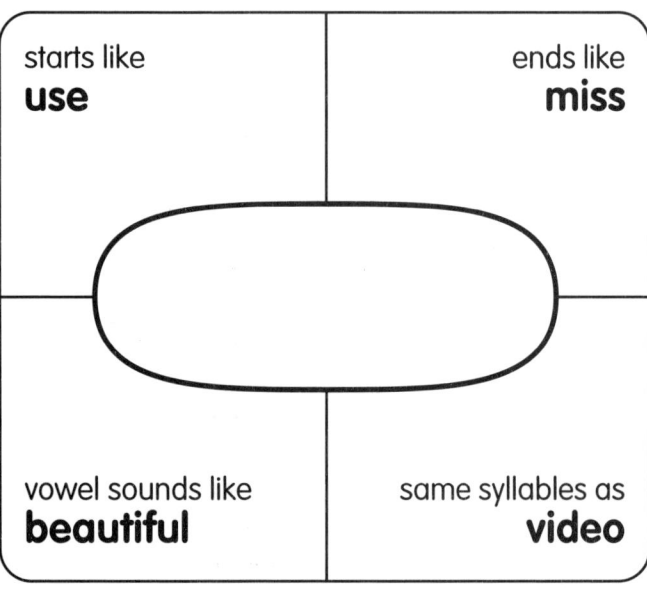

starts like **use** | ends like **miss**
vowel sounds like **beautiful** | same syllables as **video**

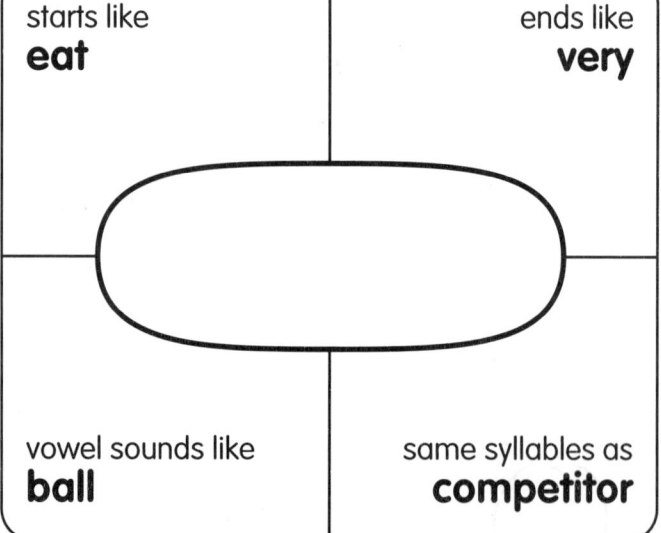

starts like **eat** | ends like **very**
vowel sounds like **ball** | same syllables as **competitor**

© Evan-Moor Corporation • EMC 8275 • Spelling Games and Activities

Past or Present?

Some words belong to the past. Other words belong to the present.
Look at the chart of spelling words. Write a word to finish each sentence.
Then circle 🕐 or ⏰ to show whether the word belongs in the present or the past.

	approach	awake	break	echo	follow	obey	speak	write
	present							
	approached	awoke	broken	echoed	followed	obeyed	spoken	wrote
	past							

After hiking all day, Jay _____awoke_____ at noon the next day.

Crash! The vase fell. It was _____broken_____.

She _____wrote_____ a poem for her best friend.

They have to _____obey_____ Grandpa's rules.

When I _____approach_____ a street, I look both ways before I cross.

Big, empty houses often _____echo_____.

Jana still hasn't _____spoken_____ to Chandra.

My dog _____followed_____ me to school yesterday.

98   Spelling Games and Activities • EMC 8275 • © Evan-Moor Corporation

Oh, Yes!

Read the clue. Write **o**, **oa**, **oe**, or **ow** to finish the answer.

I rhyme with the word **tomato**.  p__o__tat__o__	You can set me, meet me, or score me. 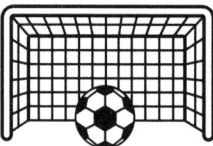 g__oa__l	I am a tube hidden in your body.  thr__oa__t
Sometimes I repeat, sometimes I rhyme.  p__o____e__m	I have a lot of salt, but you can't eat me.  __o__cean	I'm the opposite of **yesterday**.  t__o__m__o__rr__o__w
I'm the boldest, but with one letter missing.  __o__ldest	In a computer, I'm a set of directions.  pr__o__gram	I hold the key to something that is mine.  __ow__ner

Red Light, Green Light

Some of the sentences below are missing apostrophes! Read each sentence. If the sentence is correct, **color the traffic light green**. If it is missing an apostrophe, **color the traffic light red**. Then write the correct spelling word in the last column.

1. Read the sentence.	2. Is there an **apostrophe** missing from this sentence?	3. Write the spelling word with its apostrophe.
My little sisters havent figured out how to tie their shoes yet.	🔴 ⚪ ⚪	haven't
I'd walk to school with my friends, but they've already left.	⚪ ⚪ ⚪	
Jameela said she would be here at seven oclock.	⚪ ⚪ ⚪	
Were going to see a movie tonight.	⚪ ⚪ ⚪	
Lizzie, don't you want to eat lunch with us?	⚪ ⚪ ⚪	
There isnt enough time for another game.	⚪ ⚪ ⚪	
That sentence doesn't make any sense.	⚪ ⚪ ⚪	
Did you know theres a picnic in the park tomorrow?	⚪ ⚪ ⚪	
I wont forget to call you.	⚪ ⚪ ⚪	

Better Together! Use this worksheet with week 5 of *Building Spelling Skills*, grade 5

Name _____

Red Light, Green Light, *continued*

1. Read the sentence.	2. Is there an **apostrophe** missing from this sentence?	3. Write the spelling word with its apostrophe.
You arent tired yet, are you?	○ ○ ○	
They couldn't wait to go camping!	○ ○ ○	
Youre right about that math problem.	○ ○ ○	
Kazuko didnt finish her dinner tonight.	○ ○ ○	
Whose cats and dogs are these?	○ ○ ○	
Ill be more excited about moving when we're done.	○ ○ ○	
Its not likely to rain tomorrow.	○ ○ ○	
Whos hungry for lunch?	○ ○ ○	
Ive written the assignment in my notebook.	○ ○ ○	

Spot the Schwa

Most words with more than one syllable have a schwa sound. Read each word in the box and decide which vowels are making each schwa sound. Circle the vowels. Then write each word in its Schwa Zone. If a word has more than one schwa, write the word in each zone. Use a different color for each zone

| apply | diagram | higher | idea |
| license | silent | variety | widest |

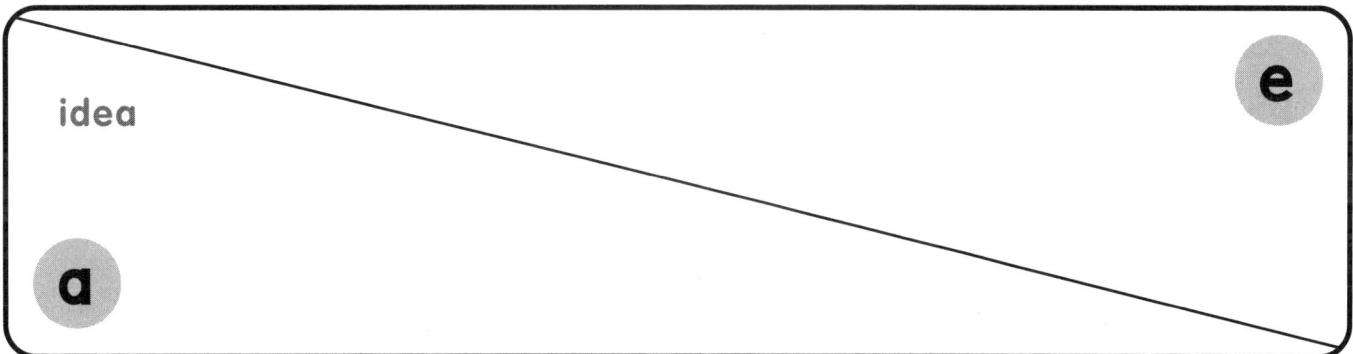

Eye on the Vowel

There are several ways to spell a **long i** sound. Most spellings use an **i** or a **y**. Read each word and circle the vowel making the **long i** sound. Write the word in the side with the vowel that makes the **long i**. Use a different color for each side.

| buy | inquire | knight | myself |
| python | quite | rhyme | smiling |

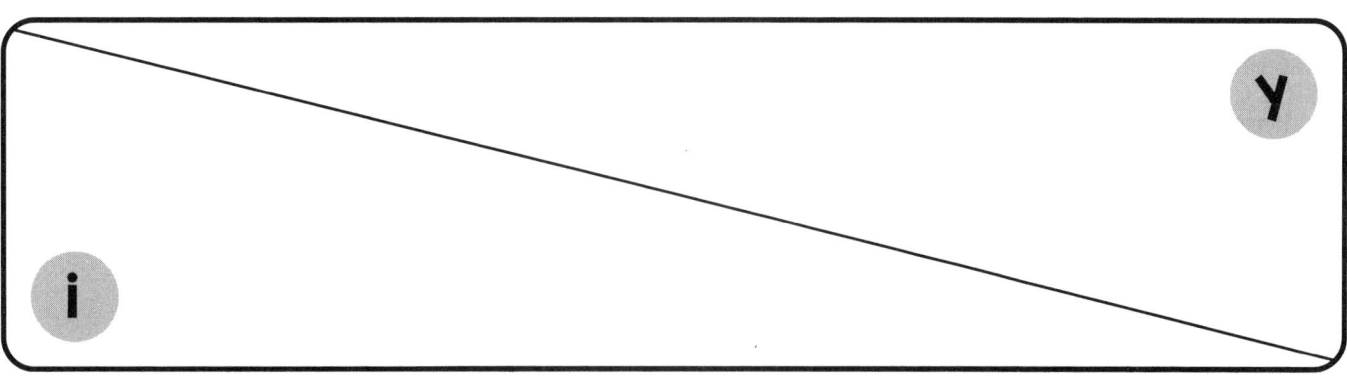

Better Together! Use this worksheet with week 6 of *Building Spelling Skills,* grade 5

Name _____

Baffling Riddles

One word in each group is spelled incorrectly. Find the word and spell it correctly in the spaces below the group. Then write the numbered letters in the matching spaces of the riddle to answer it.

What word contains 26 letters but only has three syllables?

___ ___ ___ ___ ___ ___ ___ ___
 1   2   3   4   5   6   7   8

1. higher, silent, lieing

   ___ ___ ___ ___ ___
       2

2. lisense, rhyme, widest

   ___ ___ ___ ___ ___ ___ ___
                           7

3. apply, variaty, myself

   ___ ___ ___ ___ ___ ___ ___
                   8

4. bie, I'm, idea

   ___ ___
    6

5. inquire, quite, pithon

   ___ ___ ___ ___ ___ ___
    3

6. rhyme, smiling, knite

   ___ ___ ___ ___ ___ ___
                4

7. dyagram, apply, variety

   ___ ___ ___ ___ ___ ___ ___
            5   1

© Evan-Moor Corporation • EMC 8275 • Spelling Games and Activities

Better Together! Use this worksheet with week 7 of *Building Spelling Skills*, grade 5

Name _____

New School

Benjamin just finished his first day at a new school. Look at the map of the school. His path to the bus goes through all the words that have the same vowel sound as **school**. Draw a line from Benjamin to the bus.

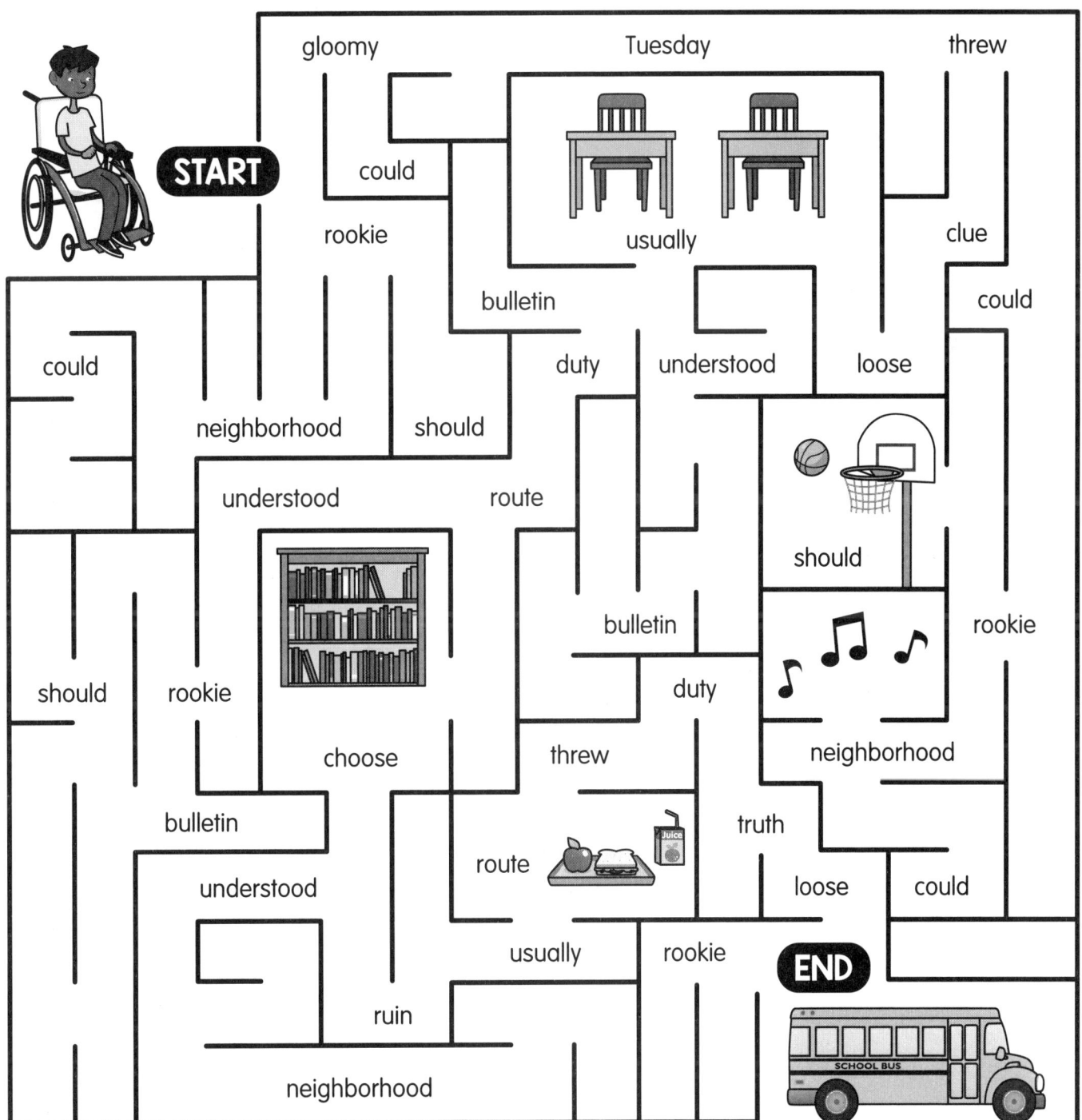

Better Together! Use this worksheet with week 7 of *Building Spelling Skills,* grade 5

Name _____

Text Truths

Medhi and Gabrielle are texting each other. Write the spelling words to complete the text messages.

| gloomy | neighborhood | rookie | school |
| should | Tuesday | understood | usually |

Hey, where were you _____ night?!
You're _____ at the weekly _____ potluck.

I was too tired after _____.

Is something wrong? You've been kind of _____ lately. You can always tell me the truth.

I guess…I just feel like a total _____ on the volleyball team. I didn't want to see the rest of my team at the potluck. But I _____ have told you that. I know you would have _____.

Thanks for telling me now! I think you're doing great on the team. And you know I always have your back.

Better Together! Use this worksheet with week 8 of *Building Spelling Skills*, grade 5

Name _____

Violet Vowels

The words below are missing their vowels! Luckily, there are vowels growing on the violet petals. Finish the words using the vowels on the violets. Cross off each vowel after you use it.

1. av____ ____d

2. empl____ ____

3. spr____ ____t

4. m____ ____nt____ ____n

5. ____ ____rselv____s

6. b____ ____nd____r____

7. ch____ ____c____

8. ____ ____st____r

9. gr____ ____nd

10. s____m____h____w

Silly Poems

Read the poem and look at the words below each line. Write the word that is spelled correctly to complete the poem.

A king decided to _____
(emploi, employ)

A jester he liked to _____.
(annoi, annoy)

The king would _____
(spoil, spoyl)

His tricks most _____,
(roial, royal)

And this gave the king much joy!

I was at my best friend's _____
(house, howse)

Playing with her pet mouse.

We didn't _____
(allou, allow)

It out, but _____
(somehou, somehow)

It got loose and ran up my blouse!

Have you ever eaten an _____?
(oister, oyster)

They have lots of _____.
(moisture, moysture)

If you ever have a _____,
(choice, choyce)

Eat one and you'll rejoice!

I checked each of the _____
(amounts, amownts)

Of what I'm growing in the _____.
(ground, grownd)

Of ginger, I have only an _____.
(ounce, ownce)

Of carrots, I have a whole pound!

Better Together! Use this worksheet with week 9 of *Building Spelling Skills*, grade 5

Name _____

Compound Coloring

What animal has patches of different colors? Read the word in each space. Color each space following these rules:

- Use orange for hyphenated compound words.
- Use blue for one-word compound words with 2 syllables.
- Use green for one-word compound words with 3 or more syllables.
- Use gray for two-word compound words.

Better Together! Use this worksheet with week 9 of *Building Spelling Skills*, grade 5

Name _____

Swimmer Pairs

A bunch of words have gone swimming in their own lane. But some words often swim together as a pair. Use the words to make as many compound words as you can. Write them in the box.

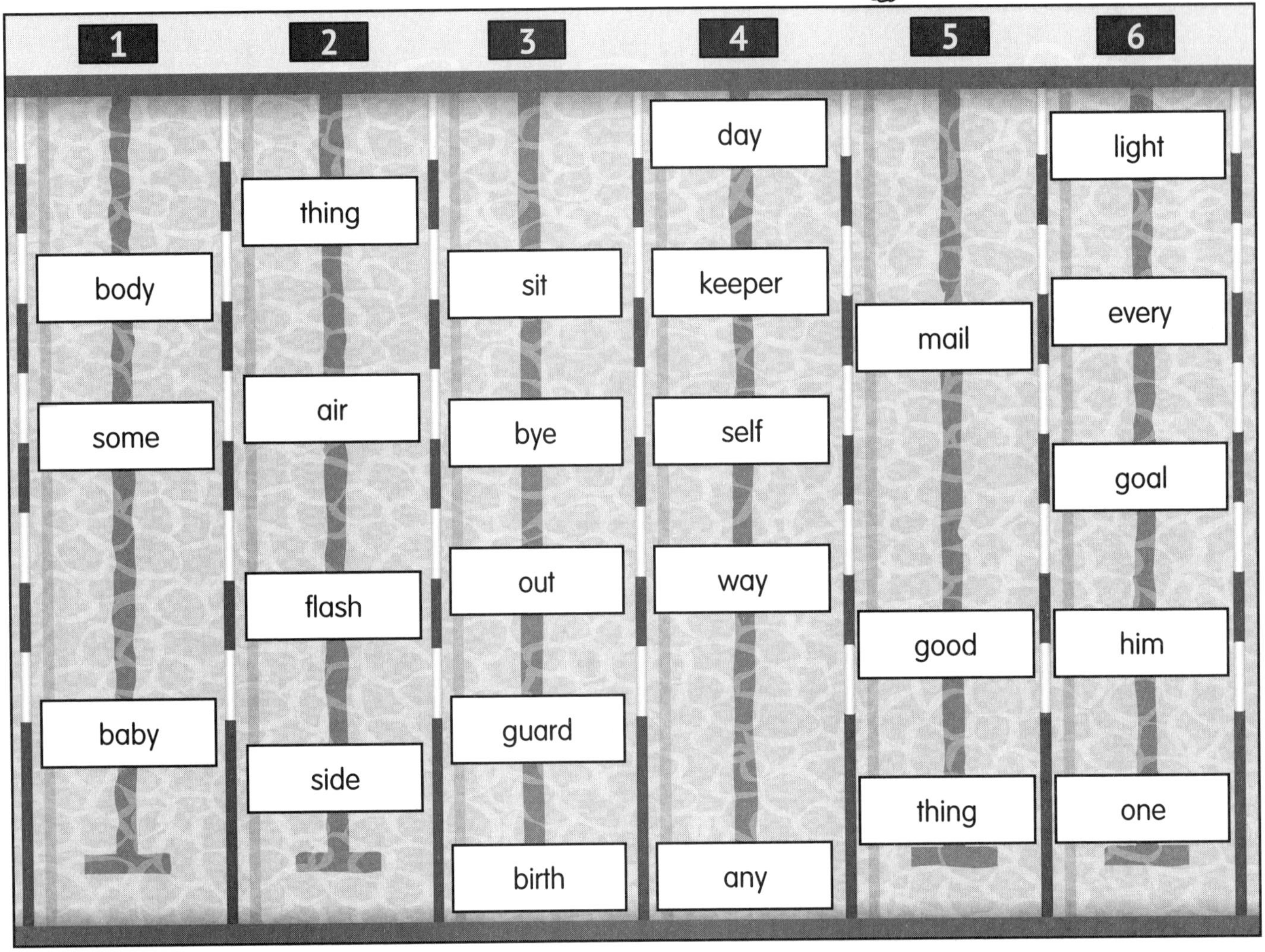

1	2	3	4	5	6
			day		light
	thing				
body		sit	keeper		every
				mail	
some	air	bye	self		
					goal
	flash	out	way		
				good	him
baby		guard			
	side			thing	one
		birth	any		

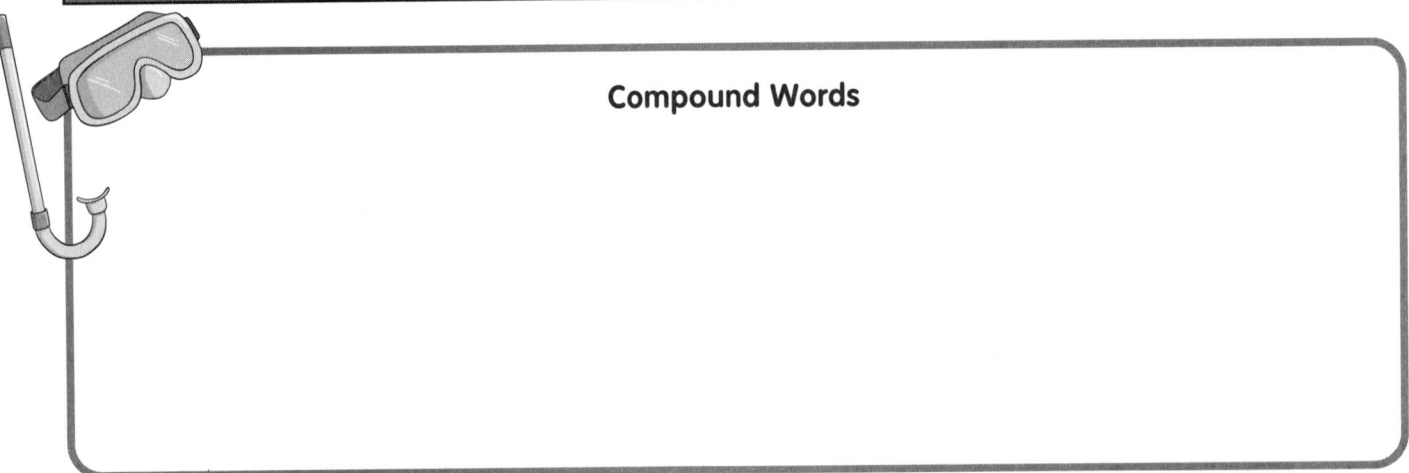

Compound Words

Puzzling Anagrams

You can change the silly phrases below to spell the words in the box.
After you unscramble each phrase, write the spelling word on the line.

> already   although   always   author
> because   brought   daughter

1. our hat   _____

2. hated rug   _____

3. sea cube   _____

4. hot laugh   _____

5. hot grub   _____

6. say law   _____

7. ear lady   _____

Better Together! Use this worksheet with week 10 of *Building Spelling Skills*, grade 5

Name _____

Hidden Message

Find 11 words in the word search that have a **short o** sound. Words may go forward, backward, up, down, or diagonally.

| awful |
| awkward |
| belong |
| called |
| drawn |
| fault |
| haul |
| lawyer |
| off |
| office |
| stalk |

F	S	E	T	C	A	Y	C	U	R	I	O	K	U	S
A	A	X	C	J	A	L	U	F	W	A	K	L	J	V
U	O	L	M	I	R	L	A	D	D	A	F	A	U	J
L	A	L	T	E	F	R	L	C	R	A	V	T	O	L
T	R	P	Y	T	U	F	M	E	K	C	G	S	V	O
B	R	W	D	C	J	W	O	W	D	W	J	W	A	N
N	A	V	H	U	D	X	B	Q	H	T	O	F	T	G
L	T	O	W	A	B	D	Z	O	D	K	F	R	W	C
F	V	M	C	M	U	F	C	U	E	A	I	I	D	B
F	B	S	F	G	Q	L	C	C	N	Z	D	J	Q	E
G	V	N	W	K	K	P	N	Z	R	W	P	S	M	L
I	X	O	F	F	R	Y	A	V	H	D	A	Z	A	O
K	M	R	J	Q	W	Z	B	M	Q	J	D	R	R	N
W	A	W	K	W	A	R	D	V	M	Q	M	P	D	G
E	Q	O	V	O	J	A	H	E	K	Q	V	J	Y	I

Now write the unused letters on the top line, starting in the left corner, in the blank spaces below. You will find a hidden message!

___ ___ ___ ___ ___ ___   ___ ___ ___ ___ ___ ___ ___

© Evan-Moor Corporation • EMC 8275 • Spelling Games and Activities

Better Together! Use this worksheet with week 11 of *Building Spelling Skills*, grade 5

Name _____

Suffix Soups

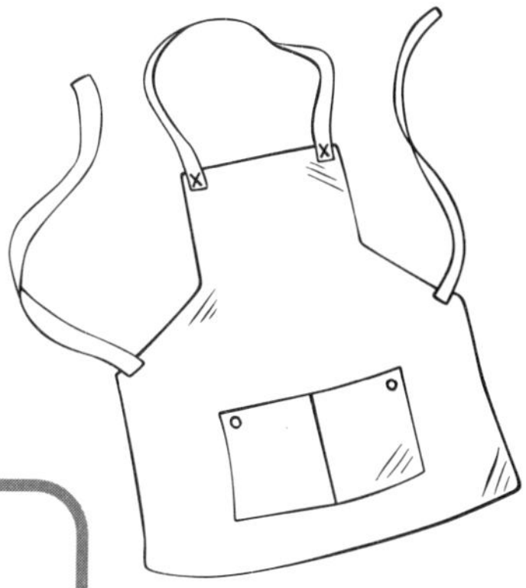

Look at the base words. For some words, you can add the ending **-ed**. You can add the ending **-est** to other words. Add the correct ending to each word and write it in the matching soup pot.

Base Words

brag   carry   finish   laugh   quick
study   surround   tiny   worry

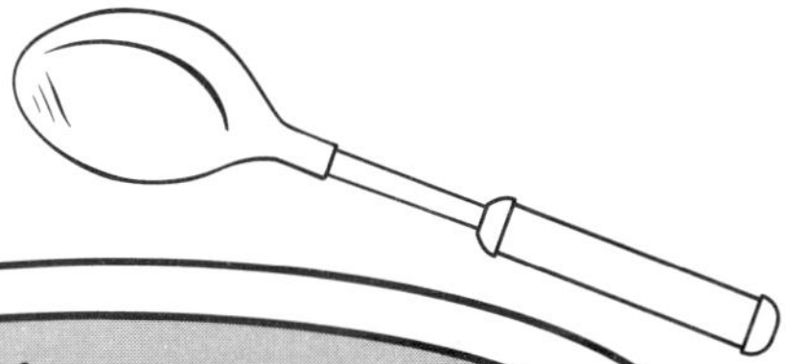

The -ed Suffix Soup

The -est Suffix Soup

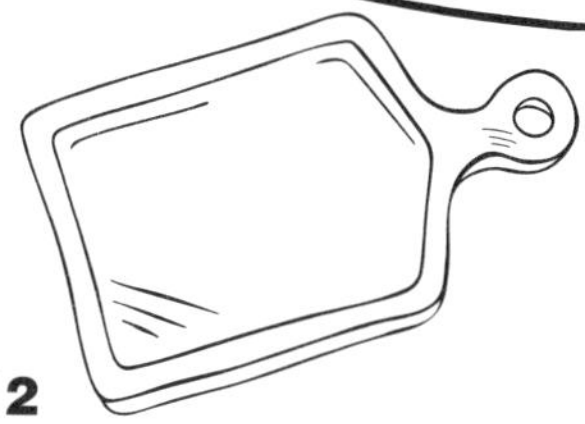

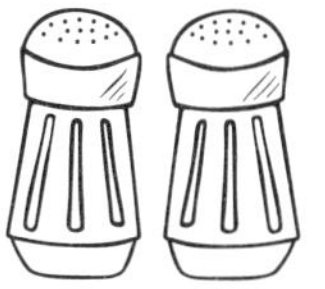

Weekend Plans

Jason and Ilhan are texting each other. Circle any misspelled words. Write them correctly below.

I'm loveing that the pool is still open so late in the year! Do you want to go swimming this Saturday?

I would, but we're travling to the mountains to go sking.

That sounds exiting! I'd like to learn to ski, but I'm much weeker on cold snow than in warm water.

I'm just begining to go down a slope. I've been doing cross-country, where we ski across flat land. It's easier, but fewer people do it, so it's lonelyer.

Well, have fun! I look forward to trading stories with you when you get back.

_____

Better Together! Use this worksheet with week 12 of *Building Spelling Skills*, grade 5

Name _____

Single Slice or Whole Pizza?

Some sentences need a singular noun. Other sentences need a plural noun. Look at the chart of spelling words. Write a word to finish each sentence. Then circle the correct amount of pizza to show what kind of noun each sentence needs.

 We had only one math _____ this week.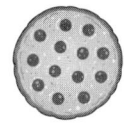

 Aliyah is my best _____ in the whole world.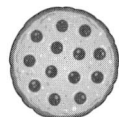

 How can you eat only a single _____?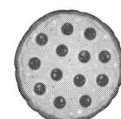

 Her passport had stamps from many _____.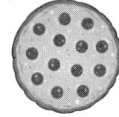

 Several students' _____ cooked for the school potluck.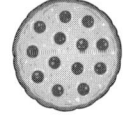

 The _____ in my family are taller than the men.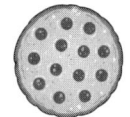

 He figured out the riddle on his first _____!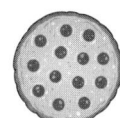

 _____ mowed the lawn and raked the _____.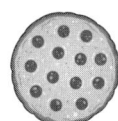

Better Together! Use this worksheet with week 12 of *Building Spelling Skills*, grade 5

Name _____

Single Piece or Whole Cake?

Some sentences need a singular noun. Other sentences need a plural noun. Look at the chart of spelling words. Write a word to finish each sentence. Then circle the correct amount of cake to show what kind of noun each sentence needs.

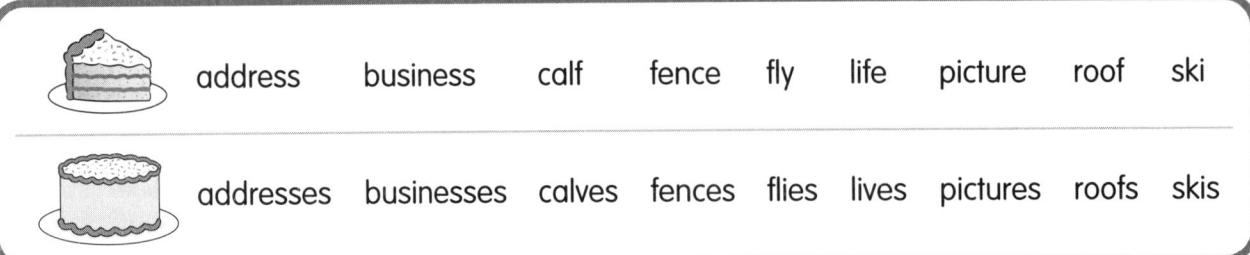

 Many _____ were saved with the firefighter's quick thinking.

 The mother cow gave birth to a _____ near the corral _____.

 The contractor put shingles on many _____ last week.

 Some _____ are closed on Sundays.

 Shoma opened the window to let out a noisy _____.

 I need Kai's new _____ so I can send him a gift.

 We put our _____ on the rack on top of the car.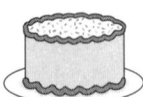

 There are family _____ all over our refrigerator.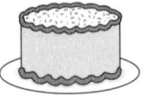

Glowing Reviews

Visitors often leave reviews for stores. Read the reviews. The underlined words are scrambled. Write them correctly below.

camera   certain   collar   color
dollar   early   earth   mayor
person   purpose   remember   surprise
urgent   wonder

Jorge ★★★★★ 1 month ago

This is my favorite ollrda store! I am always tarenic to find a prisrseu or two. They bring in new items all the time. I once found a set of bobby pins in every locor you can imagine! I even saw our town's yrmoa shopping at the store. It's popular for a reason.

_____ _____ _____ _____ _____

Yali ★★★★★ 3 weeks ago

My reacam was not working well. I was about to take a trip to dig in the ahter for dinosaur bones, so I needed neutgr help! I went to Camera City to ask about a new model. The senrpo who helped me was friendly and knew a lot about taking photos. She saved my trip!

_____ _____ _____ _____ _____

Elena ★★★★★ 5 days ago

I needed a new caolrl for my dog, Wdoren. I visited Purple Tails yarel last week with one posrepu: to buy one item. Instead, I walked out with an armful of toys! Their selection of pet items is amazing. I will rmreebme this store the next time I'm in town.

_____ _____ _____ _____ _____

Under the Microscope

Look at the letters in each spelling word. Use them to make other words. Write them on each microscope slide.

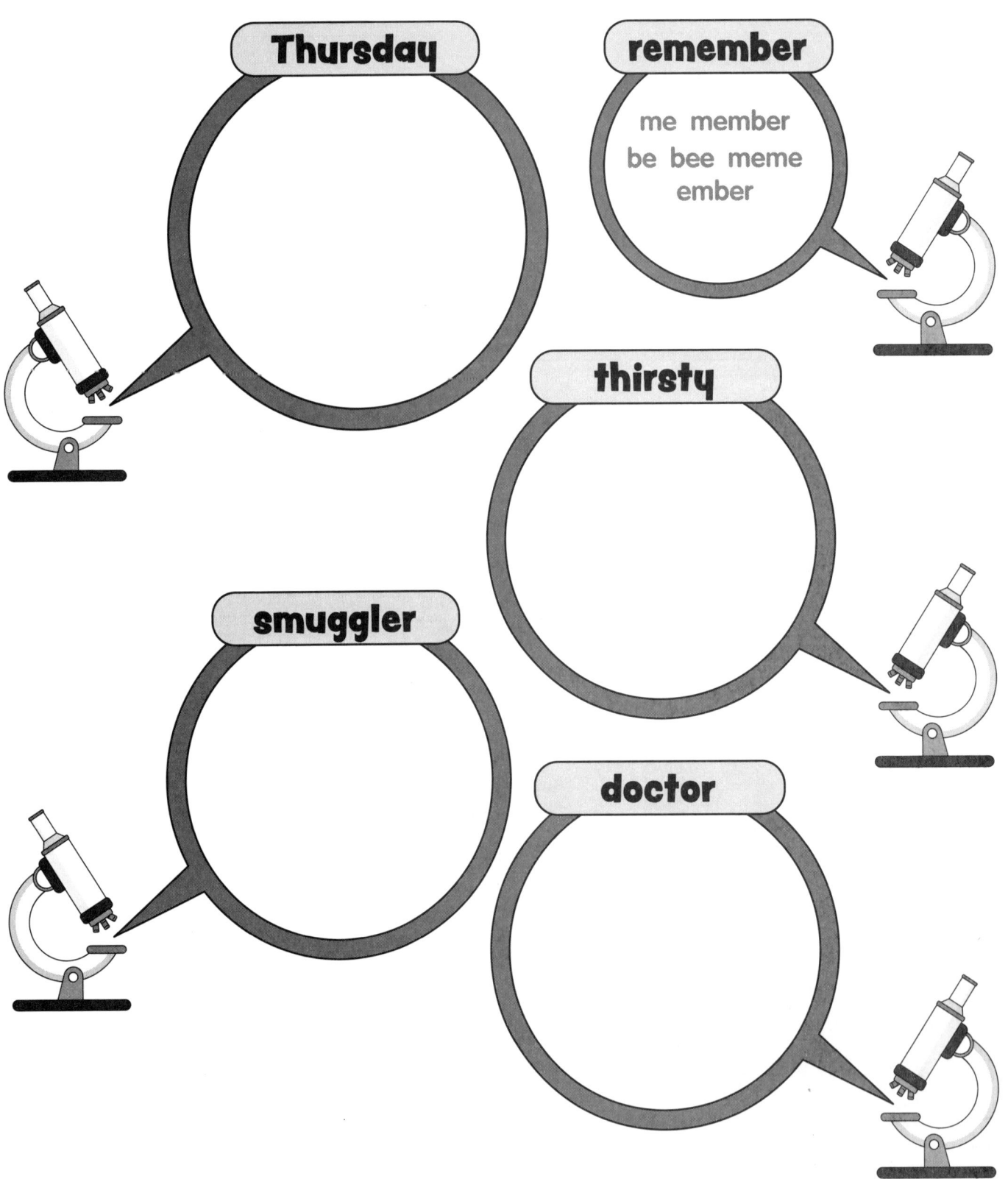

Better Together! Use this worksheet with week 14 of *Building Spelling Skills*, grade 5

Name _____

County Fair Maze

Bellamy is starting the maze at the county fair. The maze path goes through all the words that have the sound of **ar** in **care**. Draw a line from Bellamy to the end of the maze.

Better Together! Use this worksheet with week 14 of *Building Spelling Skills*, grade 5

Name _____

Postcard Pals

Hugo sent his pal, Mike, a postcard from his vacation in Spain. Write the spelling words to complete the postcard.

- area
- before
- dairy
- important
- January
- orchestra
- ordinary

Hey Mike,

　We're finally in Barcelona! Don't you wish you were here with me instead of practicing with the school _____? (I'm kidding, but I really wish you were here!)

　Mom says this is an _____ trip for us. I'm seeing the _____ where my grandparents grew up. I found out they once owned a _____ farm! We went there yesterday. I've never seen one _____.

　I just wish it was summer! It's chilly here in _____. It has been a fun trip. But I want to get back to _____ life and hang out with you!

　　　　Your friend,
　　　　Hugo

Vegetable Vowels

The words below are missing their vowels! Luckily, there are vowels growing on vegetables nearby. Finish the words using the vowels on the vegetables. Cross off each vowel after you use it.

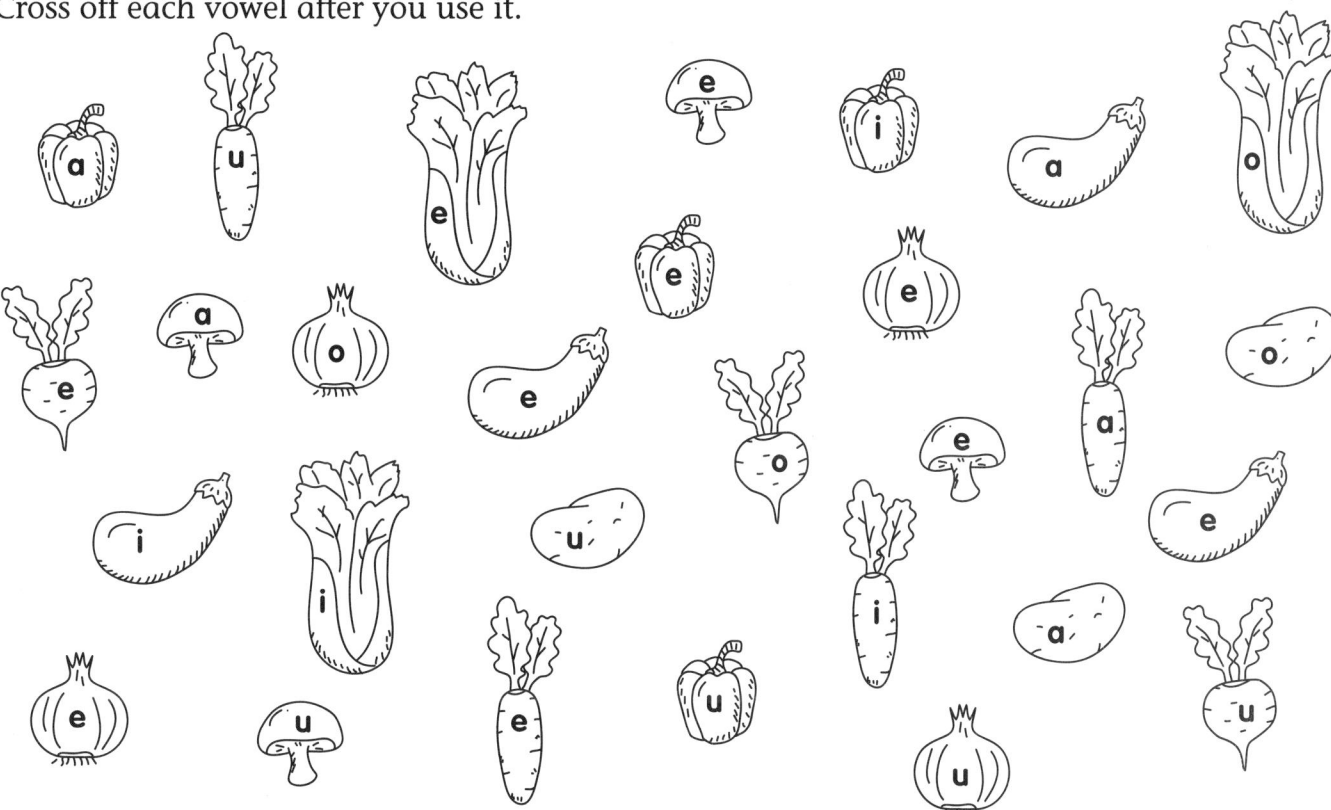

1. q __ __ t
2. h __ pp __ n
3. __ b __ t
4. p __ nct __ r __
5. __ g __ n

6. l __ ct __ r __
7. __ q __ t __ r
8. d __ ff __ r __ nt
9. s __ c __ nd
10. r __ g __ n

Mind-Boggling Riddles

One word in each group is spelled incorrectly. Find the word and spell it correctly in the spaces below the group. Then write the numbered letters in the matching spaces of the riddle to answer it.

What type of room has no doors and no windows?

___ ___ ___ ___ ___ ___ ___ ___ ___
 1   2   3   4   5   6   7   8   9

1. kompare, happen, again

   ___ ___ ___ ___ ___ ___ ___
        7   9

2. quartar, second, other

   ___ ___ ___ ___ ___ ___ ___
            3

3. along, about, dozyn

   ___ ___ ___ ___ ___
            8

4. animle, equator, quiet

   ___ ___ ___ ___ ___ ___
                2

5. puncture, allgibra, lecture

   ___ ___ ___ ___ ___ ___ ___
                        1

6. region, again, uther

   ___ ___ ___ ___ ___
                6

7. second, thowsend, different

   ___ ___ ___ ___ ___ ___ ___ ___
        5   4

Better Together! Use this worksheet with week 16 of *Building Spelling Skills*, grade 5

Name _____

Stay Cool

What refreshments would you like? Read the word in each space. Color each space following these rules:

- Use yellow for words with the **ch** consonant digraph.
- Use blue for words with the **th** consonant digraph.
- Use pink for words with the **wh** consonant digraph.
- Use green for words with the **sh** consonant digraph.

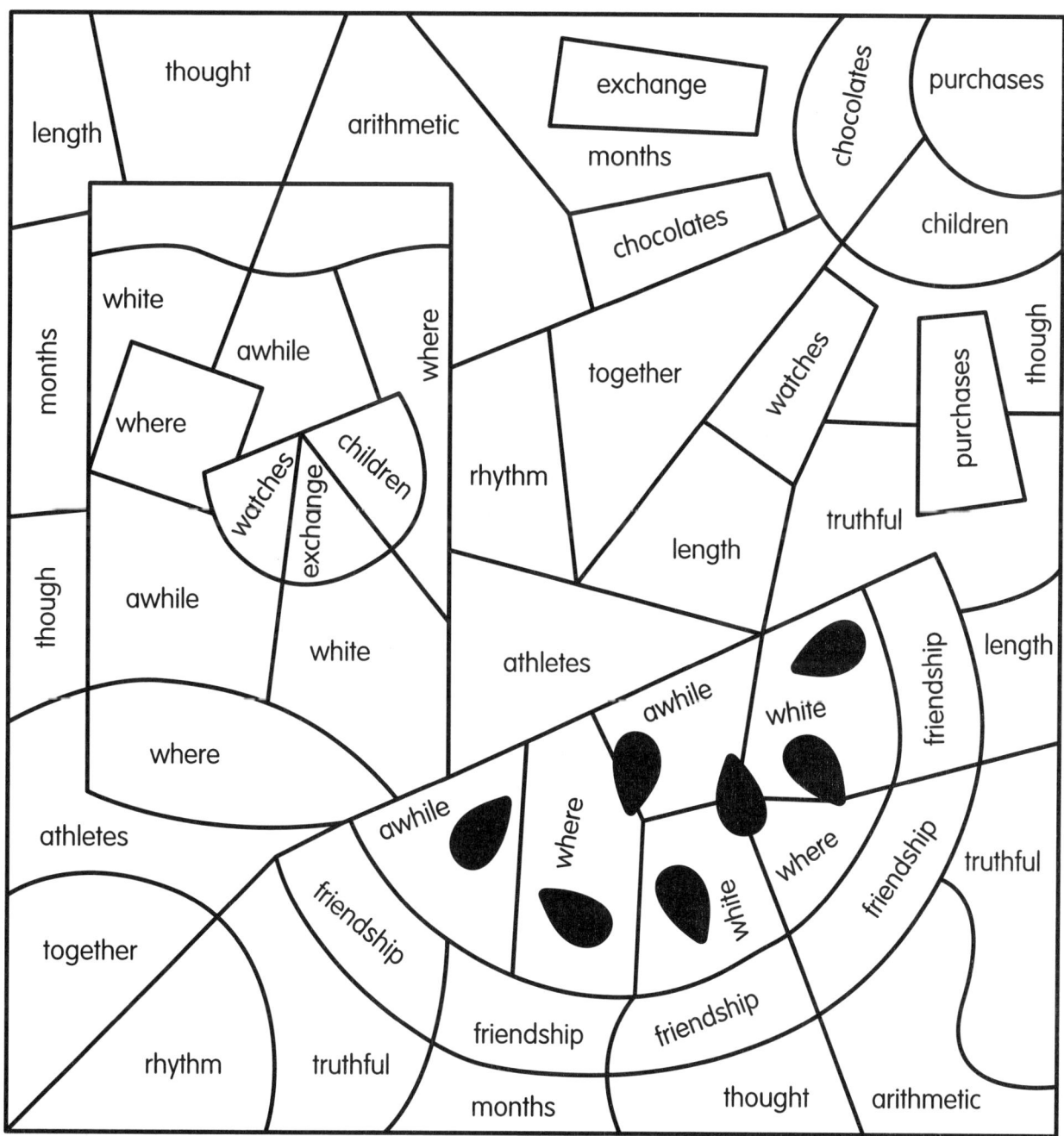

122   Spelling Games and Activities • EMC 8275 • © Evan-Moor Corporation

Better Together! Use this worksheet with week 16 of *Building Spelling Skills*, grade 5

Name _____

Use Your Clues

Look closely at the starting, ending, and vowel sounds of the clue words in the example. They describe a mystery word in the box. The mystery word will have the same sounds, but the spelling may be different from the clue words.

athletes	awhile	children	chocolates
friendship	thought	watches	white

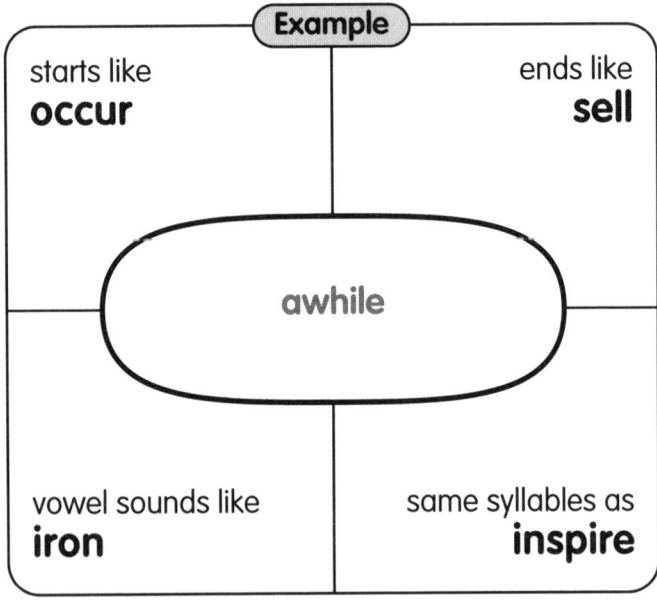

Example
- starts like **occur**
- ends like **sell**
- vowel sounds like **iron**
- same syllables as **inspire**

→ awhile

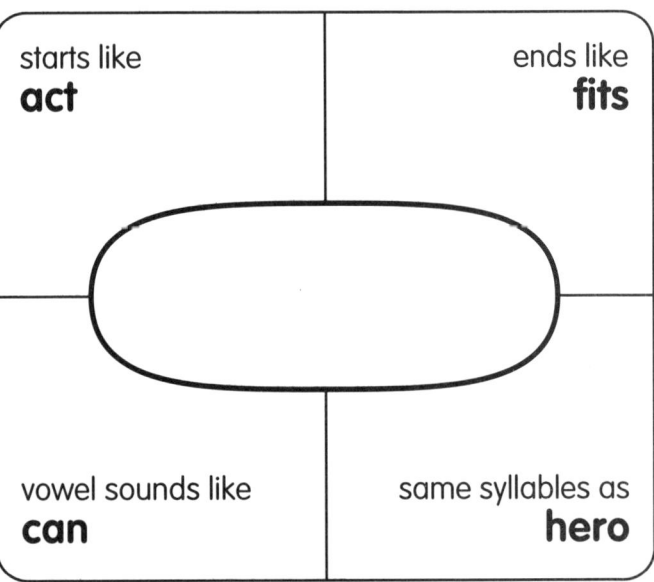

- starts like **act**
- ends like **fits**
- vowel sounds like **can**
- same syllables as **hero**

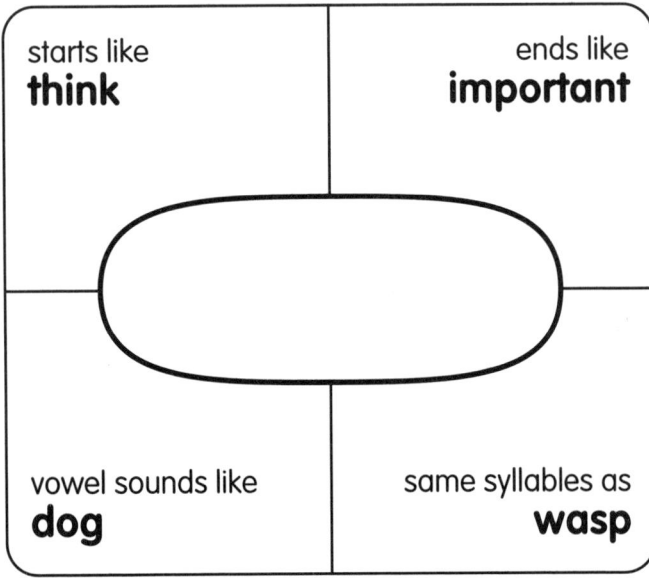

- starts like **think**
- ends like **important**
- vowel sounds like **dog**
- same syllables as **wasp**

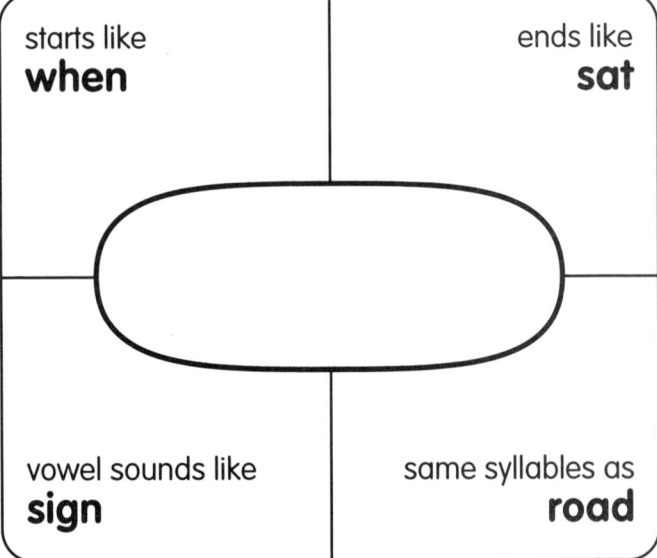

- starts like **when**
- ends like **sat**
- vowel sounds like **sign**
- same syllables as **road**

Puzzling Anagrams

You can change the silly phrases below to spell a word from the box. After you unscramble each phrase, write the spelling word on the line.

> bridge country dangerous generous
> peaceful regular segment

1. big red _____

2. cape fuel _____

3. nose guard _____

4. earl rug _____

5. cry unto _____

6. nose urge _____

7. ten gems _____

Better Together! Use this worksheet with week 17 of *Building Spelling Skills*, grade 5

Name _____

Concert Traffic

Malia is playing drums in her first concert. On her way there, she will go through the words that have a **hard c** or a **hard g** sound. Draw a line to make a path for Malia to get to the concert.

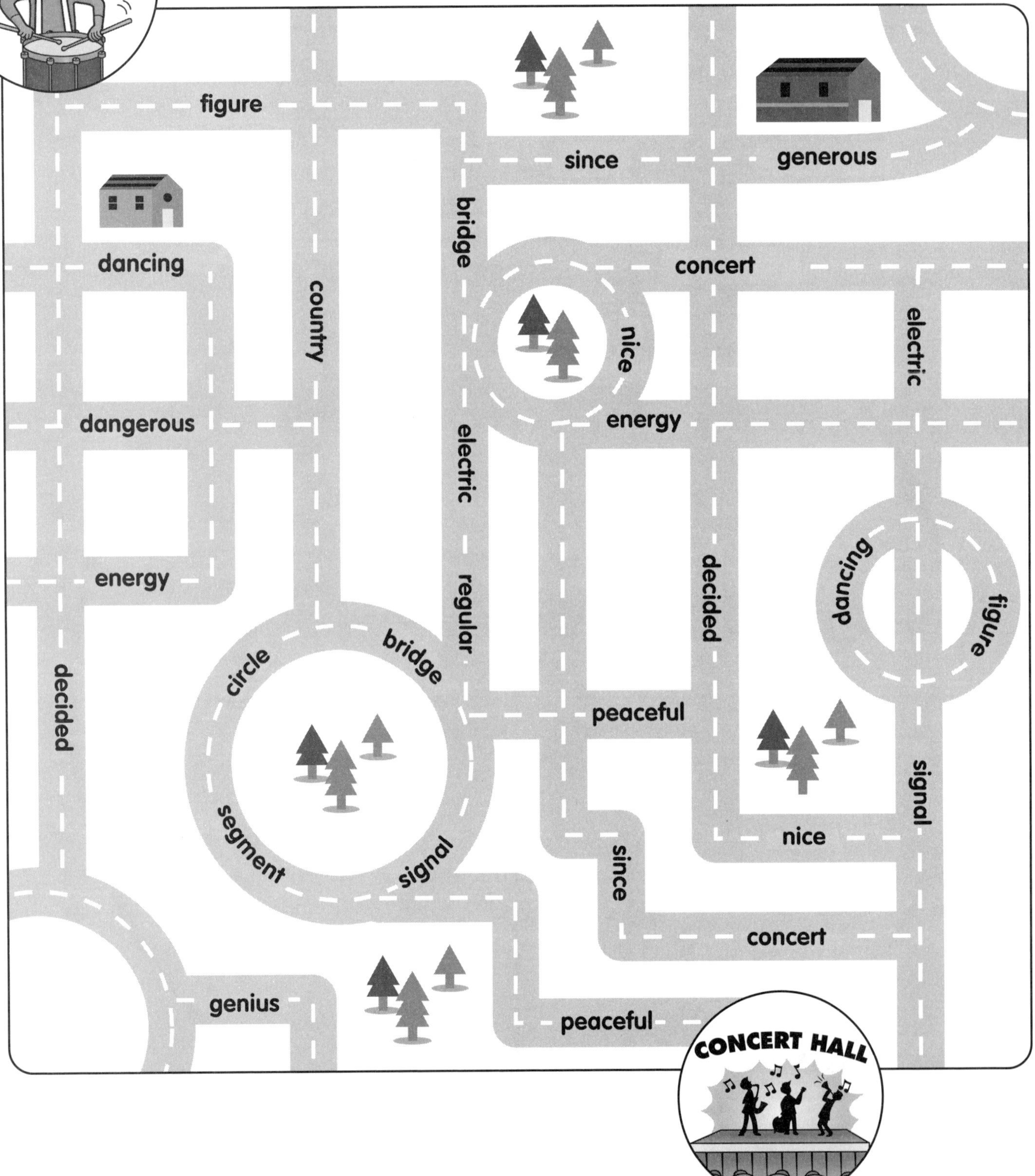

figure
since
generous
dancing
bridge
concert
country
nice
electric
dangerous
energy
electric
decided
energy
regular
dancing
decided
circle
bridge
figure
peaceful
segment
signal
nice
since
signal
concert
genius
peaceful

CONCERT HALL

Spot the Schwa

Most words with more than one syllable have a **schwa** sound. Read each word in the box and decide which vowels are making each schwa sound. Circle the vowels. Then write each word in its Schwa Zone. If a word has more than one schwa, write the word in each zone. Use a different color for each zone

| instrument | label | legal | several |
| special | telescope | terrible | towel |

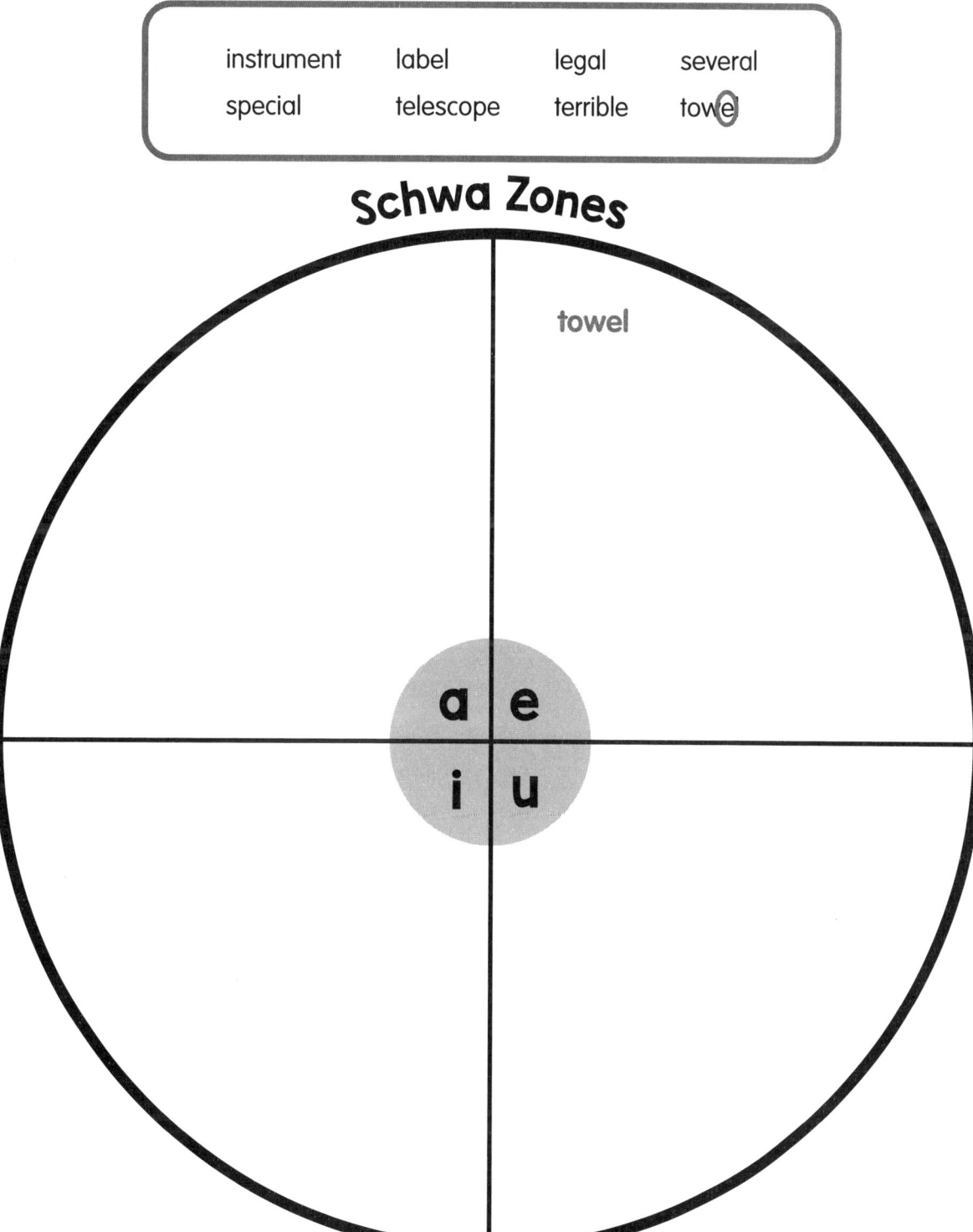

Random Riddles

Read the clue. Write a spelling word to solve the riddle.

> address   celebrate   declare   eagle   example
> frequent   instead   little   question   whole

1. I have two sets of double letters. _____

2. I have a consonant blend at both ends. _____

3. I am the opposite of big. _____

4. My **short e** sound is made by 2 vowels. _____

5. I can be written with letters or a symbol. _____

6. I rhyme with **square** and **aware**. _____

7. My **long e** sound is made by 2 vowels. _____

8. I contain another word for **test**. _____

9. My middle syllable has a schwa sound. _____

10. I have a silent consonant and a silent vowel. _____

Better Together! Use this worksheet with week 19 of *Building Spelling Skills*, grade 5

Name _____

Hide and Seek

Find 12 words in the word search that have **ei** or **ie**. Words may go forward, backward, up, down, or diagonally.

- Find 5 words that have **ei**. Circle them in blue.
- Find 7 words that have **ie**. Circle them in red.

| field | fierce | hurried | neither | piece | receive |
| receiving | siege | their | tried | weigh | worries |

F	F	G	N	I	V	I	E	C	E	R	D	R	E	I
I	A	H	U	R	R	E	I	D	J	I	N	O	C	L
E	L	M	K	F	N	S	G	U	O	T	C	D	I	A
L	G	T	H	B	D	C	E	H	I	H	R	E	E	V
D	Y	R	F	L	O	H	U	R	R	I	E	D	V	A
H	R	I	I	I	F	O	U	E	M	E	Q	U	I	D
I	S	E	D	K	E	T	R	H	N	R	W	E	N	F
T	F	D	O	R	I	R	A	T	P	O	L	N	G	O
W	N	G	R	A	R	E	C	I	E	V	E	L	I	W
Y	I	H	M	I	C	E	U	E	T	E	O	R	D	F
H	E	E	N	D	E	V	O	N	I	G	D	A	U	L
U	T	O	G	S	E	I	R	R	O	W	P	H	S	H
C	H	I	B	H	S	E	F	L	G	H	O	I	R	G
R	E	S	P	I	E	C	E	O	R	I	E	I	T	I
Y	R	H	A	P	E	E	S	W	V	G	I	J	D	E
A	W	T	T	Z	S	R	T	H	E	I	R	G	O	W

128   Spelling Games and Activities • EMC 8275 • © Evan-Moor Corporation

Better Together! Use this worksheet with week 19 of *Building Spelling Skills*, grade 5

Name _____

Homework Help

Uma and Felix are texting each other. Write the spelling words to complete the text messages.

| having | hurried | neither | planned |
| tired | trying | weighs | writing |

Hey, have you finished _____ your history assignment? I'm _____ a hard time with it.

I've been _____ to get it done all day. I _____ to go to the pottery studio this afternoon. That's not happening, though.

Are you feeling _____? You usually finish essays fast.

My dog got out and hasn't come home yet. It's hard for me to focus when a problem _____ on my mind. I feel kind of _____ to get the essay done.

It sounds like _____ of us is doing well with this assignment. Why don't I come over and help you look for your dog? I could use a break.

© Evan-Moor Corporation • EMC 8275 • Spelling Games and Activities

Suffix Salads

The words in the box have an **-ly** or **-ness** ending. Look at each word. If the word is spelled correctly, write it in the correct suffix salad.

angrily	angryly	darkily	darkness	exactily	exactly
friendily	friendly	happily	happyly	happiness	happyness
honestly	honestness	kindily	kindness	loneliness	lonleyness
saddness	sadness	speedily	speedyly	weakily	weakness

The -ness Suffix Salad

The -ly Suffix Salad

Better Together! Use this worksheet with week 20 of *Building Spelling Skills*, grade 5

Name _____

Look Closer!

Look at the letters in each spelling word.
Use them to make other words.
Write them on each magnifying glass.

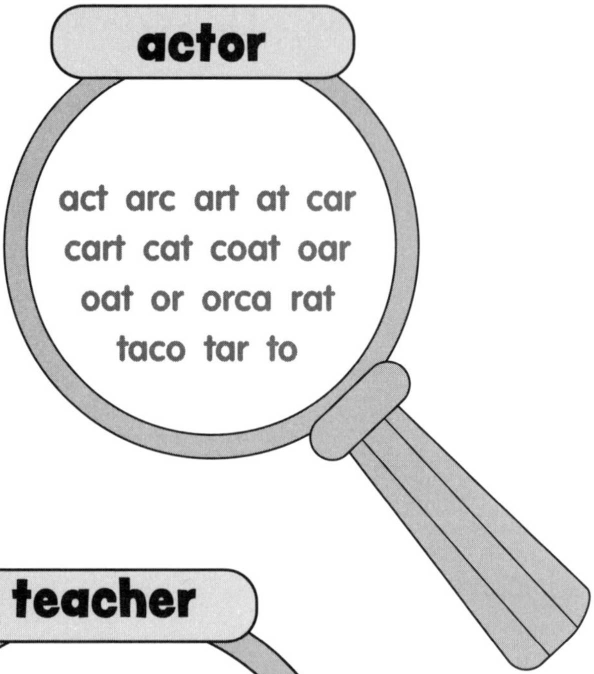

actor

act arc art at car
cart cat coat oar
oat or orca rat
taco tar to

biologist

teacher

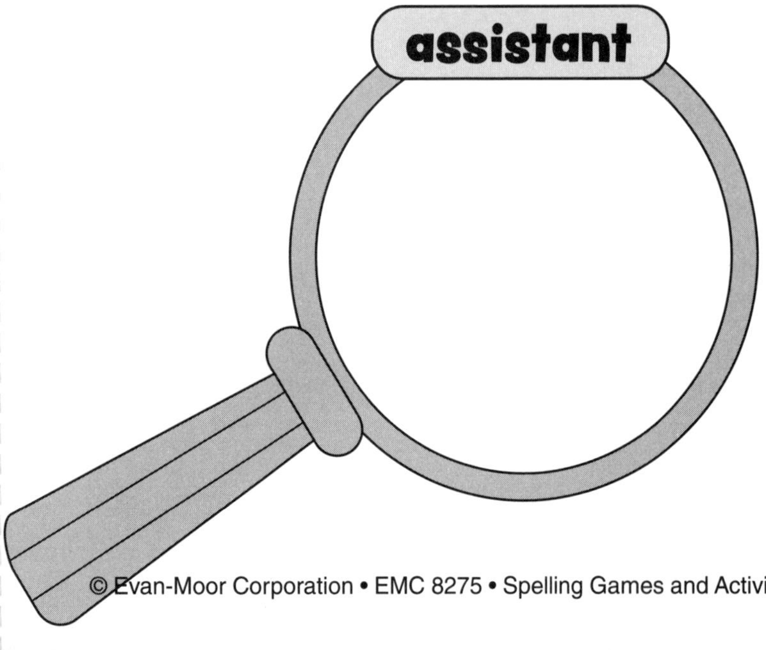

assistant

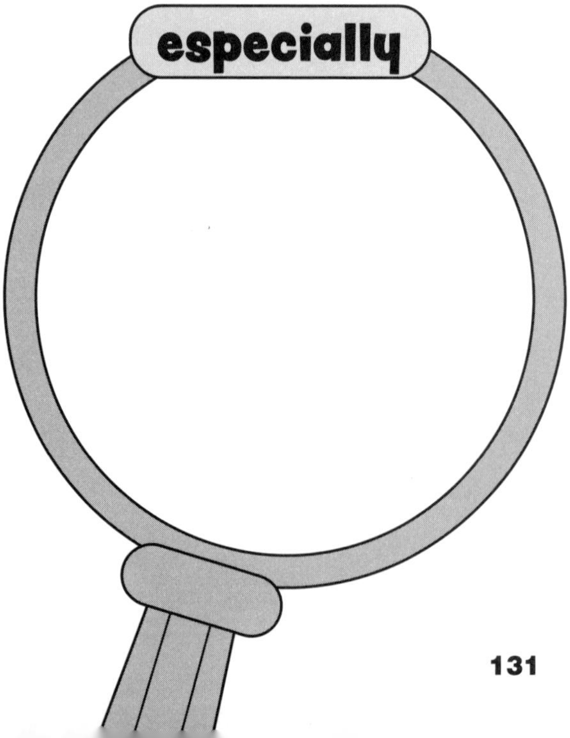

especially

© Evan-Moor Corporation • EMC 8275 • Spelling Games and Activities

Red Light, Green Light

Some of the sentences below are using incorrect homophones. Read each sentence. If the sentence is correct, **color the traffic light green**. If you find an incorrect homophone, **color the traffic light red**. Then write the correct homophone in the last column.

1. Read the sentence.	2. Is there an **incorrect homophone** in this sentence?	3. Write the correct homophone.
Grandpa is going on a **crews** to Antarctica!	🔴 ⚪ ⚪	cruise
Rebecca is **heir** to the Matterhorn fortune.	⚪ ⚪ ⚪	
We have a new **principle** at our school.	⚪ ⚪ ⚪	
The clock strikes on the **hour**.	⚪ ⚪ ⚪	
We **new** that it was too late to save the apple trees.	⚪ ⚪ ⚪	
I'd like to have **too** slices of pizza.	⚪ ⚪ ⚪	
She has **close** in every color of the rainbow.	⚪ ⚪ ⚪	
This theatre production has a **seen** with no dialogue.	⚪ ⚪ ⚪	
The dog ran **threw** the meadow over there.	⚪ ⚪ ⚪	

Better Together! Use this worksheet with week 21 of *Building Spelling Skills,* grade 5

Name _____

Red Light, Green Light, *continued*

1. Read the sentence.	2. Is there an **incorrect homophone** in this sentence?	3. Write the correct homophone.
The teacher read the book **allowed** to the class.	○ ○ ○	
She will **write** an e-mail to Nonna on Sunday.	○ ○ ○	
There was a **shoot** for garbage where we stayed in England.	○ ○ ○	
The two submarine **crews** worked together.	○ ○ ○	
Their going to take me to their hometown next week.	○ ○ ○	
We're traveling to the **Isle** of Skye in Scotland soon.	○ ○ ○	
She was a beloved queen during her **rain**.	○ ○ ○	
Fairness is an important **principal** to students.	○ ○ ○	
This file needs only one **bite** of storage space.	○ ○ ○	

Puzzling Anagrams

You can change the silly phrases below to spell a word from the box.
After you unscramble each phrase, write the spelling word on the line.

| amusement | arrangement | plentiful | predicament | skillful |
| thoughtless | wasteful | wonderful | worthless | |

1. full silk _____

2. rapid cement _____

3. owl refund _____

4. tuna memes _____

5. saw flute _____

6. unfelt lip _____

7. great manner _____

8. howl rests _____

9. ghost hustle _____

Baffling Riddles

One word in each group is spelled incorrectly. Find the word and spell it correctly in the spaces below the group. Then write the numbered letters in the matching spaces of the riddle to answer it.

Every person has me, and no one can escape me. What am I?

___ ___ ___ ___ ___ ___ ___
 1   2   3   4   5   6   7

1. govurment, successful, wonderful

   ___ ___ ___ ___ ___ ___ ___ ___ ___ ___
            6

2. reckless, careless, feerless

   ___ ___ ___ ___ ___ ___ ___
        1

3. skillful, thotful, excitement

   ___ ___ ___ ___ ___ ___ ___ ___
        3

4. plentiful, sucessful, punishment

   ___ ___ ___ ___ ___ ___ ___ ___ ___ ___
                    2

5. worthliss, reckless, amusement

   ___ ___ ___ ___ ___ ___ ___ ___ ___
    7

6. wonderful, useless, waistful

   ___ ___ ___ ___ ___ ___ ___
        4

7. excitement, predikamint, careless

   ___ ___ ___ ___ ___ ___ ___ ___ ___ ___ ___ ___
                    5

Laces and Letters

The **sh** sound fell out of the words below! Luckily, there are **sh** sounds on the shoe rack. Finish the words using the letters on the shoes. Cross off each letter or pair of letters after you use it.

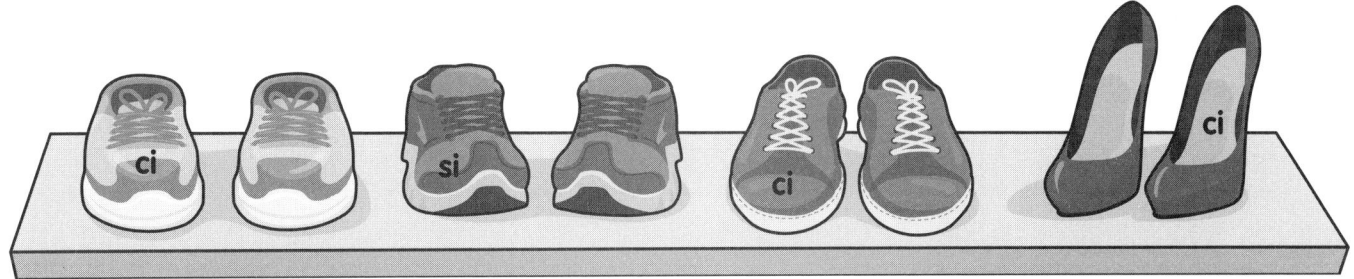

1. pa____ence

2. musi____an

3. ____ugar

4. constitu____on

5. physi____an

6. conclu____on

7. constella____on

8. gla____er

9. mi____ion

10. offi____al

Thank-You Letter

Carolina wrote to her uncle. Read her e-mail. The underlined words are scrambled. Write the words correctly below.

> addition   caution   fiction   occasion
> position   shoes   sure   tension

New message

To: Tío Ricardo
Subject: Thank you!

Dear Tío Ricardo,

Thank you so much for the new pair of hiking <u>soshe</u>!

I love going for hikes with our dog, Teddy, but Mamá said I need to use <u>cnutaio</u> if I go on the trails without proper footwear. I'll still be careful, for <u>erus</u>, but I'm excited to try them out soon! It is the perfect <u>oantidid</u> to my closet. Thanks again!

My graduation from fifth grade was a special <u>saoinocc</u>. Mamá baked my favorite cookies, and we went to a movie. I wish you'd been there!

I'm still playing soccer, but my <u>nitoiosp</u> on the team has changed. I'm now the goalkeeper. When I'm not on the field, I am still writing. Mamá says my <u>itfoicn</u> stories have a lot of <u>stennio</u>!

Love, Carolina

Better Together! Use this worksheet with week 24 of *Building Spelling Skills*, grade 5

Name _____

Silent Sails

Some letters fell out of the words below! Luckily, there are sailboats with letters sailing nearby. Finish the words using the letters on the sails. Cross off each letter after you use it.

1. ans____ ____r

2. w____is____le

3. ____res____le

4. do____ ____h

5. t____ni____t

6. ta____k____ng

7. ____n____t

8. ____on____r

9. lis____ ____n

10. scra____ ____

Better Together! Use this worksheet with week 24 of *Building Spelling Skills*, grade 5

Name _____

Postcard Pals

Milo sent his pal Sebastian a postcard from his time exploring the West Coast. Write the spelling words to complete the postcard.

climb	design	half
islands	knapsack	limbs
unknown	wrong	

Hey Sebastian,

　Well, we are two weeks into our time exploring the San Juan _____! We're staying in Friday Harbor right now.

　Mom made sure to _____ our trip so we had time to relax. _____ the time, we walk around and look for ice cream to eat!

　Yesterday we went on a _____ up Young Hill.

Dad pulled muscles in two _____ on the hike! So today, we are taking it easy and checking out a lighthouse.

　By the way, I was _____ thinking I needed a huge suitcase.

I'm so happy you told me to use my red _____ instead. It is so much easier to carry!

　I'd better get ready now for tomorrow's _____ adventures!

　　　　See you soon, Milo

© Evan-Moor Corporation • EMC 8275 • Spelling Games and Activities　　139

Prefix Pies

Look at the base words. Each word can take one of these prefixes: **re-**, **dis-**, **mis-**, or **il-**. Add the correct prefix to each word and write it in the matching prefix pie.

Base Words

call	build	write	legible	honest	behave	connect
use	spell	agree	legal	fortune	approve	appoint

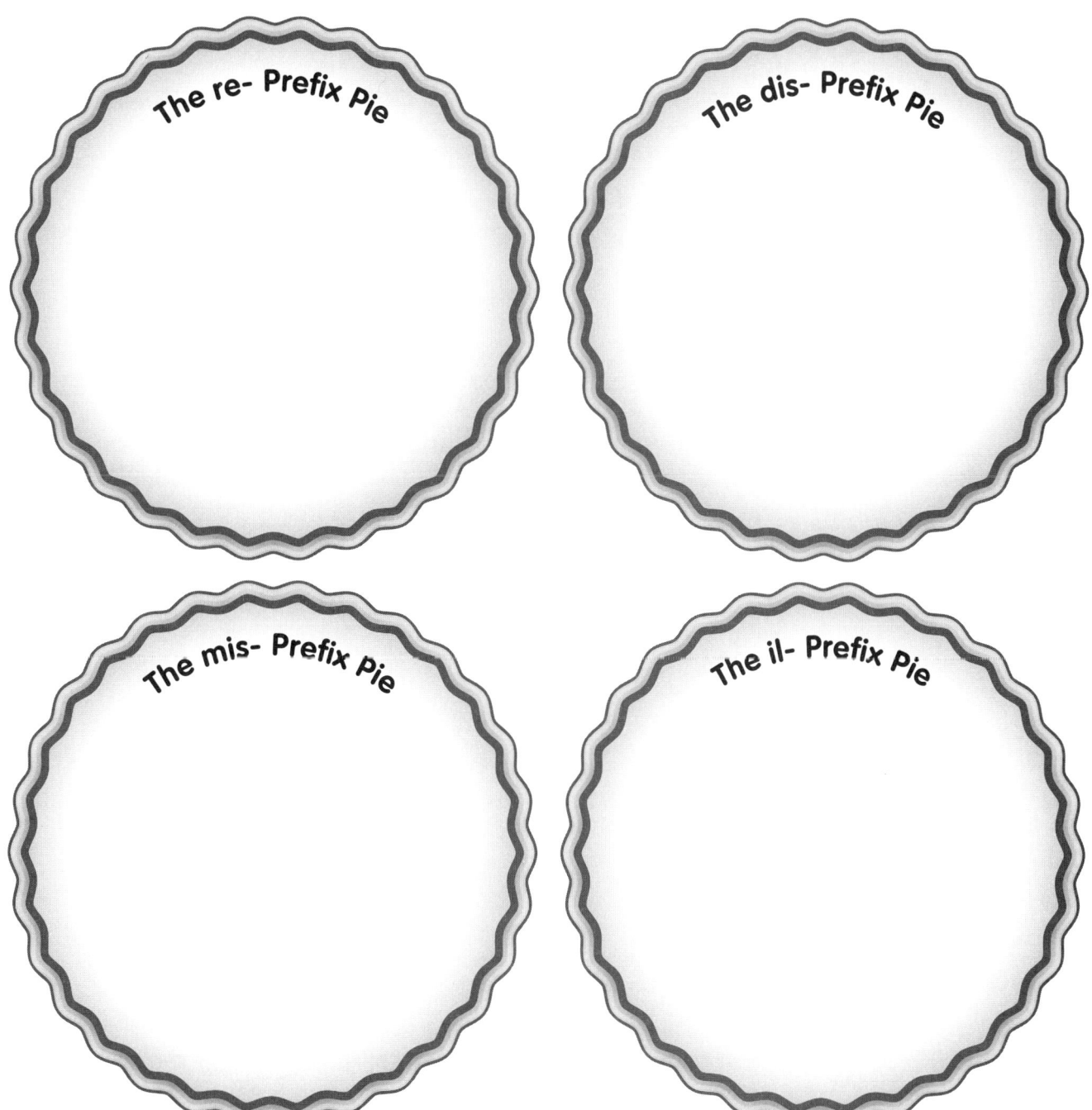

Use Your Clues

Look closely at the starting, ending, and vowel sounds of the clue words in the example. They describe a mystery word in the box. The mystery word will have the same sounds, but the spelling may be different from the clue words.

| disappear | disappoint | misbehave | misfortune |
| misspell | misunderstand | reappear | recover |

Example

starts like **route**	ends like **sugar**
reappear	
vowel sounds like **fear**	same syllables as **entertain**

starts like **rack**	ends like **doctor**
vowel sounds like **run**	same syllables as **assistant**

starts like **many**	ends like **rebuild**
vowel sounds like **camp**	same syllables as **automobile**

starts like **donkey**	ends like **art**
vowel sounds like **boy**	same syllables as **understood**

Marvelous Muffins

Look at the different spellings of the **f** sound. Write each word in the correct muffin.

briefly	cough	enough	festival	few	fluid
fourth	fragile	Friday	nephew	paragraph	pharmacy
physical	roughest	stuffed	telephone	triumph	trophy

Concealed Creature

What animal is hiding in this picture? Read the word in each space. Color each space following these rules.

- Use orange for words with the prefix **pre**-.
- Use green for words with the prefix **un**-.
- Use light brown or gray for words with the prefix **im**-.
- Use dark brown for words with the prefix **in**-.

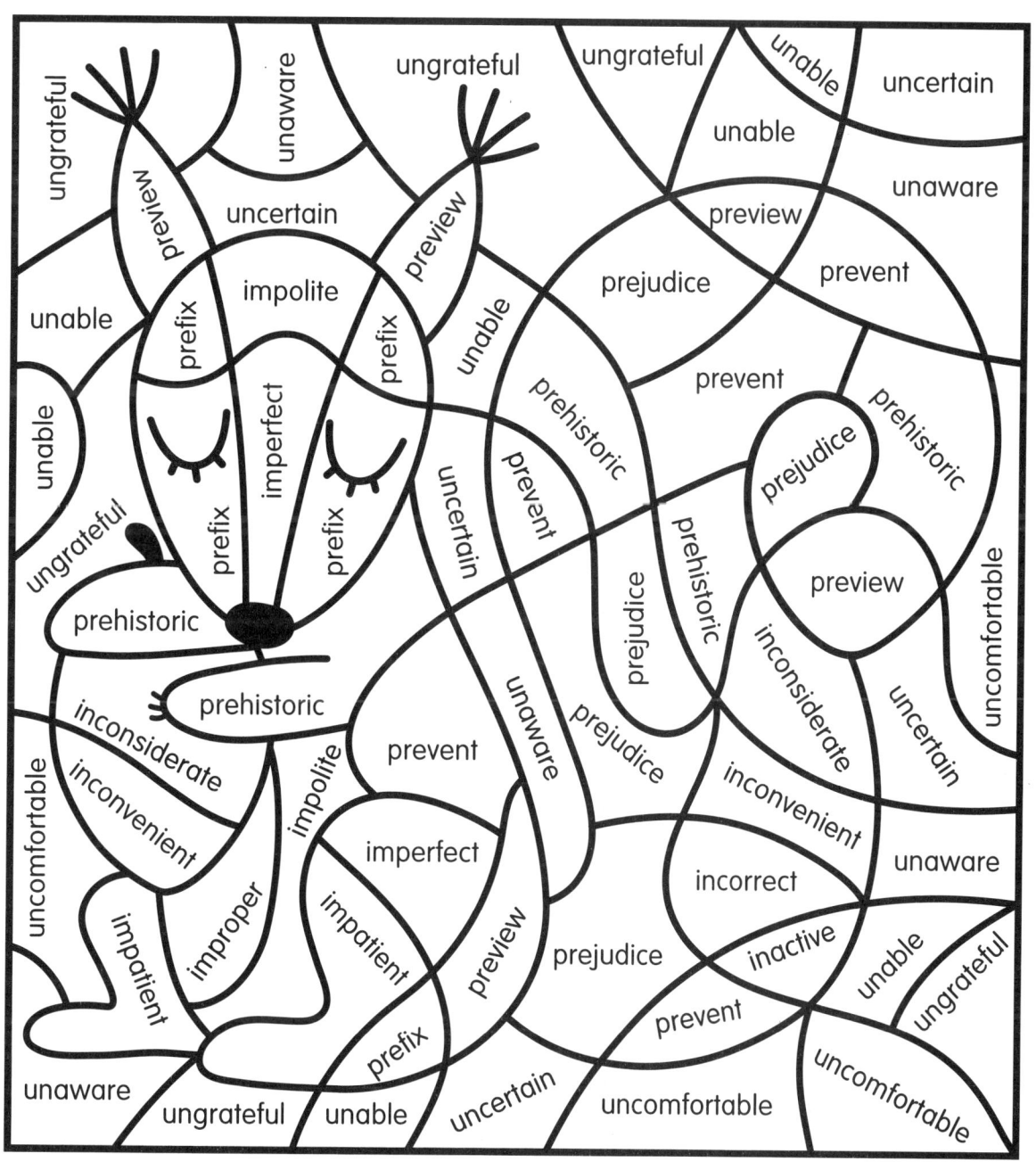

Better Together! Use this worksheet with week 27 of *Building Spelling Skills*, grade 5

Name _____

Hot or Not?

Some words are antonyms of each other, such as "ripe" and "unripe." Look at the chart of antonyms. Write a word to finish each sentence. Then circle  or to show what kind of adjective each sentence needs.

☀	❄
active	inactive
certain	uncertain
comfortable	uncomfortable
considerate	inconsiderate
grateful	ungrateful
historic	prehistoric
perfect	imperfect
polite	impolite

 _____ times ended when people began to write.

 My mom reminded me to speak in a _____ way to others.

 This scratchy chair is _____.

 My abuela and I go for a walk every day to stay _____.

 He is _____ about whether he should try out for the play.

 Even the most beautiful flower is _____.

 That _____ driver turned right in front of my bike!

 I'm so _____ to have friends who support me.

Better Together! Use this worksheet with week 28 of *Building Spelling Skills*, grade 5

Name _____

Spot the Schwa

Most words with more than one syllable have a **schwa** sound. Read each word in the box and decide which vowels are making each schwa sound. Circle the vowels. Then write each word in its Schwa Zone. If a word has more than one schwa, write the word in each zone. Use a different color for each zone

| autograph | bicycle | encyclopedia | geography | ge(o)gist |
| geometry | photograph | portable | telegraph | |

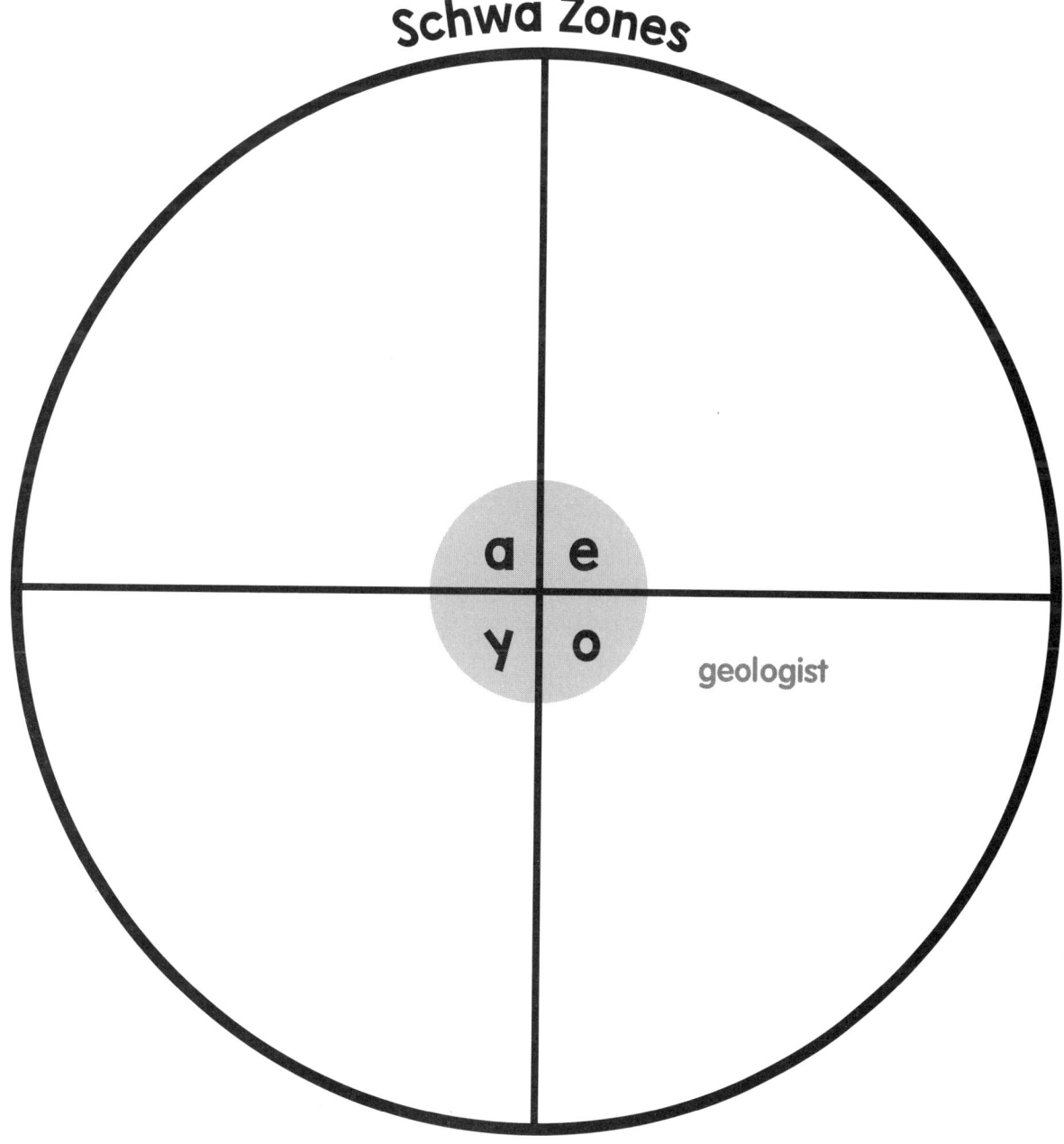

Better Together! Use this worksheet with week 28 of *Building Spelling Skills*, grade 5

Name _____

Secret Proverb

Find 12 words in the word search that have a Greek or Latin root or affix. Words may go forward, backward, up, down, or diagonally.

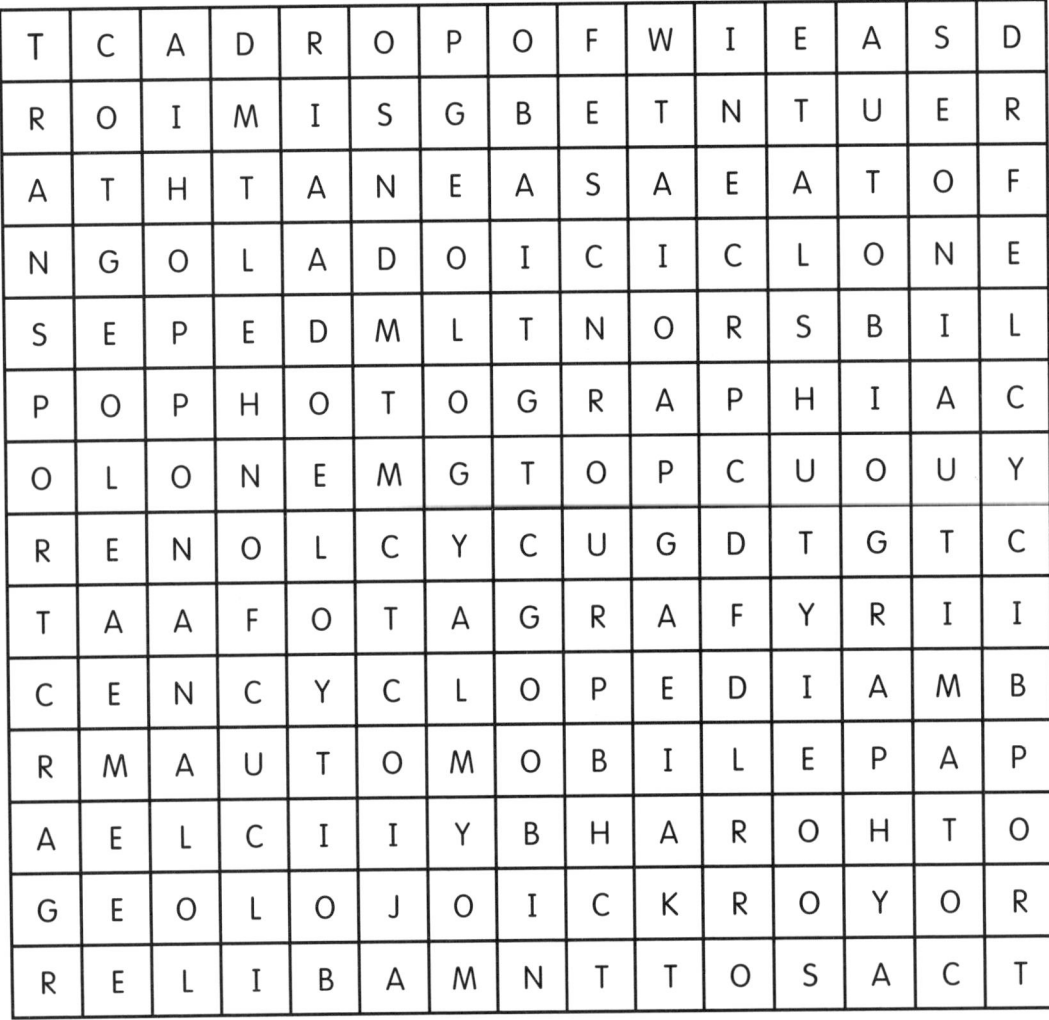

action
autobiography
automatic
automobile
bicycle
cyclone
enact
encyclopedia
geology
import
photograph
transport

Now write the unused letters in the blank spaces below, starting in the top left corner. You will find a secret Greek proverb!

___ ___ ___ ___ ___ ___   ___ ___ ___ ___ ___ ___

___ ___ ___ ___ ___ ___ ___ ___ ___ ___

___ ___ ___ ___ ___ ___ ___ ___ ___ .

© Evan-Moor Corporation • EMC 8275 • Spelling Games and Activities

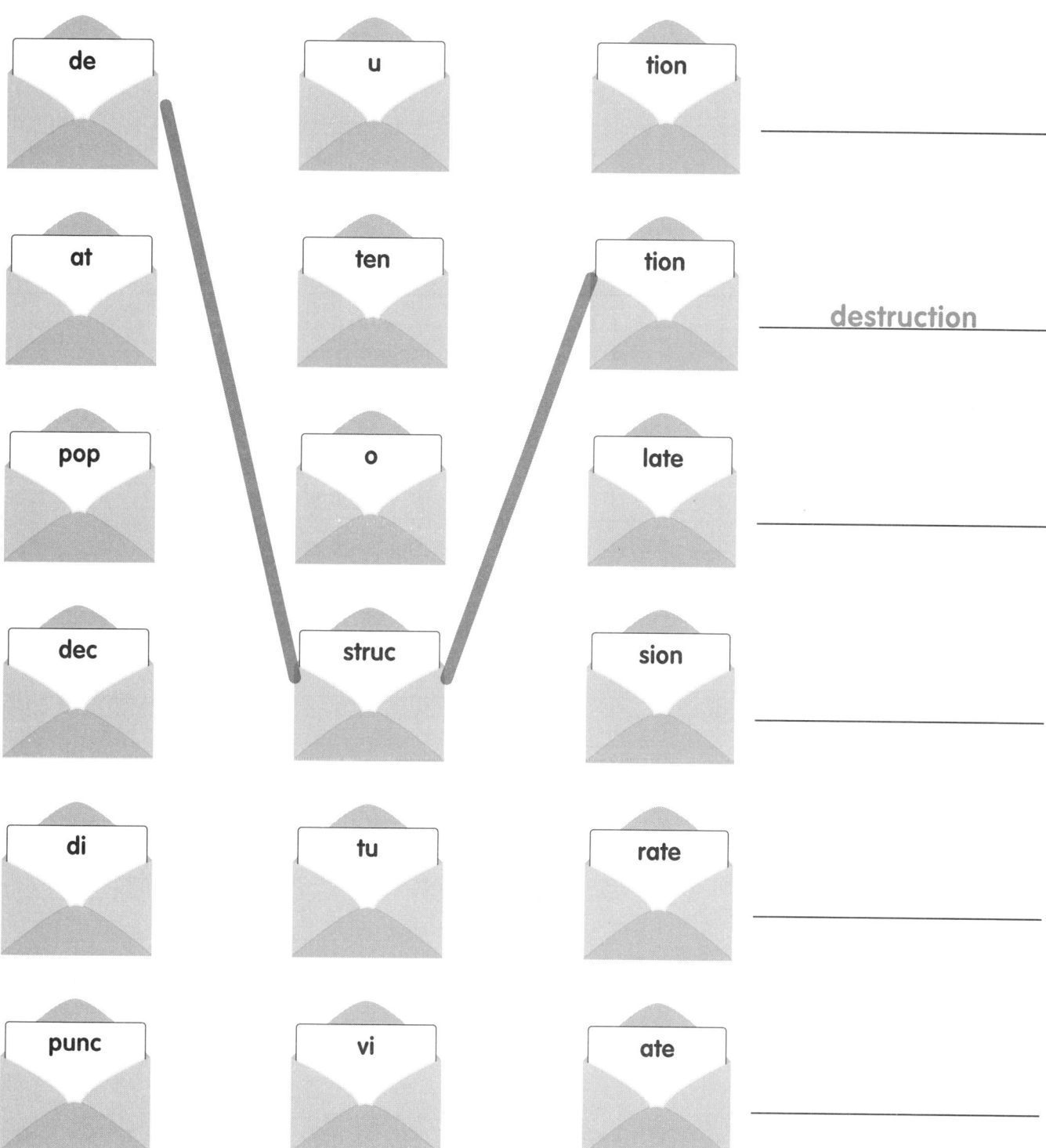

Riddle Me Right

Unscramble each word. Then write the numbered letters in the matching spaces of the riddle to answer it.

What type of band can never play a tune?

___ ___ ___ ___ ___ ___ ___ ___ ___ ___ ___ ___ !
 1   2   3   4   4   5   6   4   7   8   9

1. soriednipct   ___ ___ ___ ___ ___ ___ ___ ___ ___ ___ ___
                          2

2. ounacntiutp   ___ ___ ___ ___ ___ ___ ___ ___ ___ ___

3. oceirtanod   ___ ___ ___ ___ ___ ___ ___ ___ ___ ___
                              1

4. sdtruetc   ___ ___ ___ ___ ___ ___ ___ ___
                              6

5. iocnietnf   ___ ___ ___ ___ ___ ___ ___ ___ ___
                                              8

6. dirtaismen   ___ ___ ___ ___ ___ ___ ___ ___ ___ ___
                  7

7. dieecsbr   ___ ___ ___ ___ ___ ___ ___ ___
                              4

8. etdnat   ___ ___ ___ ___ ___ ___
                              9

9. ipolutaopn   ___ ___ ___ ___ ___ ___ ___ ___ ___ ___
                      3

10. eidivd   ___ ___ ___ ___ ___ ___
                          5

administer
attend
decoration
describe
description
destruct
divide
infection
population
punctuation

Life in New Zealand

Bobby needs help proofreading his social studies assignment. Circle any misspelled words. Write them correctly below.

New Zealand is an interesting place. It has a modern civilazation, but it still honors its Māori culture. They use modern tecknology, but sometimes they sudsitute old methods. For example, they use energy from underground for heating and cooking. In some places, the high underground tempriture makes bubbling mud pools that people like to soak in. However, the mud pools smell like rotten eggs!

New Zealand has many animals that aren't found anywhere else. Many of their birds, such as the kiwi and the takahē, have an unusual charicturistic: they can't fly. There is also an anfibian called Archey's frog that lived with the dinosaurs!

The small island country has a lot of agriculchure. There are so many sheep that you have to multiply the number of people by 5 to see how many! New Zealand maniufactures a lot of meat products and wool clothing.

_____ _____ _____ _____

_____ _____ _____ _____

Puzzling Anagrams

You can change the silly phrases below to spell a word from the box.
After you unscramble each phrase, write the spelling word on the line.

> agriculture   atmosphere   environment   equation
> intersection   representative   semicircle   vertical

1. men inventor   _____

2. a quiet no   _____

3. reverse patient   _____

4. cruel guitar   _____

5. cat liver   _____

6. insert notice   _____

7. mother peas   _____

8. slicer mice   _____

Spelling Strategies
How to Spell Hard Words

There are so many words that it would be hard to memorize them all! It helps to have a plan when you are writing. Here are ways to figure out how to spell words that you don't know.

👂🖐️	**Say the word.** Listen to the sounds and syllables. (Ask yourself) What do I hear? What do I know?
i before e except after c	**Think about rules or patterns** using the sounds you heard. (Ask yourself) Is there a rule or pattern I can follow?
-ight family might right bright tight knight slight tonight eyesight	**Think about similar words** that you know how to spell. (Ask yourself) Does it rhyme with another word? Is it part of a word family?
un|ex|pect|ed	**Divide the word.** Break compound words into two parts. Divide between prefix, base word, and suffix. Divide it into syllables. (Ask yourself) How can I divide it into smaller pieces?
success sŭk sĕs' to do well	**Try to spell the word.** You can try different ways. (Ask yourself) Does it look right? Is it in the dictionary?

Spelling Strategies
Spelling Vowel Sounds

Every word has a vowel sound. There are different kinds of vowel sounds. Look at the chart to find the kind you hear in a word.

I hear a short vowel sound.

Write the letter you hear:

gr**a**ph, h**e**lp, dr**i**nk, s**o**ng, m**u**ch, s**y**mphony

Or try a digraph:

h**ea**d, fr**ie**nd, t**ou**ch, **aw**ful

I hear a long vowel sound.

Write the letter you hear and a silent **e** after the consonant:

s**a**ve, th**e**se, pr**i**ce, cl**o**se, c**u**be

Or try a digraph:

br**ea**k, afr**ai**d, tod**ay**, w**ei**gh, pr**ey**, rec**ei**ve, n**ie**ce, **ea**sy, c**oa**st, thr**ou**gh, s**ui**t, r**oo**m

I hear a schwa sound.

Any vowel can have a schwa sound:

alive, happ**e**n, tenn**i**s, **o**'clock, min**u**te

Make a guess and write the word:
- See if it looks right.
- Check the dictionary.
- Make up a memory clue.

I hear something else.

R-controlled vowels are not short or long. Write the vowel that sounds closest.

h**ar**d, pref**er**, b**ir**d, doct**or**, t**ur**n

Diphthongs are letter pairs that make two sounds together:

v**oi**ce, l**oy**al, h**ou**se, t**ow**n

Other sounds:

c**oo**k, c**ou**ld, p**u**sh, w**a**tch

Spelling Strategies
Spelling Consonant Sounds

Every word has a consonant sound. Some consonants have two sounds. Look at the chart to find the sound you hear in a word.

 I hear a j sound.

Write a **j** most of the time:

en**j**oy, **j**ury

Write a **g** if the next sound is an **e** or **i** sound or if it is the last sound in the word:

dan**g**er, **gi**ant, chan**g**e

 I hear an s sound.

Write an **s** most of the time:

save, al**s**o, **s**urprise, a**s**k, **s**low, **s**mile, **s**nap

Write a **c** if the next sound is an **e** or **i** sound:

center, re**c**ital, accura**c**y

 I hear a k sound.

Write a **c** most of the time:

carry, be**co**me, **c**ute, **c**lean, **c**ruise, do**c**tor

Write a **k** if the next sound is an **e** or **i** sound or if it is the last sound in the word:

po**ck**et, **k**ite, ali**k**e

 I hear an f sound.

Write an **f** or **ph** at the beginning:

follow, **ph**one

Write an **f**, **ff**, or **ph** in the middle:

li**f**e, di**ff**erent, al**ph**abet

Write an **f**, **ff**, **ph**, or **gh** at the end:

proo**f**, o**ff**, gra**ph**, cou**gh**

 I hear something else.

Digraphs are letter pairs that make a new sound together:

tea**ch**er, **sh**ort, nor**th**, **wh**ere

 What am I not hearing?

Many words have **silent letters**. Some are in word families. Memorize them:

com**b**, colum**n**, **g**nat, is**l**and, lis**t**en, hal**f**, **h**our, **k**now, **w**rap

Spelling Strategies
Breaking Down Words

It is easier to spell long words when you break them into smaller pieces.

Divide compound words.
Compound words are made of two shorter words put together.

1. Say the word.

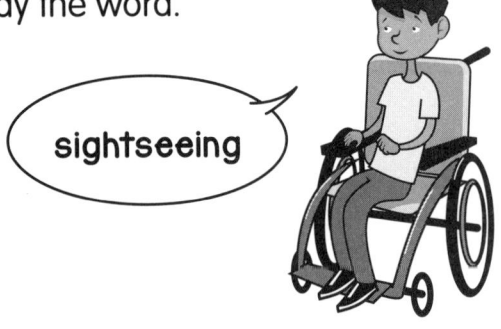

sightseeing

2. Figure out the two words that make up the compound word.

sight

seeing

3. Spell the smaller words.

sightseeing

Divide words between syllables.
Syllables are short pieces of a word. Each syllable has a vowel sound in it. Every time you say a syllable, your chin moves.

1. Say the word.

thermometer

2. Listen to each syllable. Figure out the sounds in each syllable.

ther – mom – e – ter

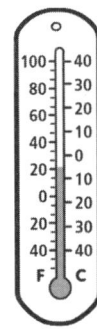

3. Spell the syllables together.

thermometer

Spelling Strategies
Using Suffixes

You can make more words by adding suffixes to the ends of words you know.

Make plural words.

Most nouns: add **s**	Nouns ending in **s, ss, sh, ch, x,** or **z**: add **es**	Nouns ending in a consonant + **y**: drop the **y**, add **ies**
shoe**s**, insect**s**, turkey**s**	bus**es**, guess**es**, wish**es**, watch**es**, box**es**, waltz**es**	cherr**ies**, stor**ies**

Make describing words.

Most words: add **er, est, ly, ful, ness, less**	Words ending in **y**: change **y** to **i** and add the suffix
hard**er**, high**est**, friend**ly**, care**ful**, great**ness**, fear**less**	happ**ier**, happ**iest**, happ**ily**, happ**iness**

Change action words.

Most verbs: add **ed** or **ing**	Verbs ending in **e**: drop the **e** and add **ed** or **ing**	Verbs ending in **y**: change **y** to **i** and add **ed**
finish**ed**, call**ing**	believ**ed**, clos**ing**	carr**ied**, suppl**ied**

Spelling Strategies
Using a Dictionary

A dictionary can tell you a lot about words. It tells you how to spell them, how to say them, and what they mean.

How to find a word

"I don't know how to spell it. How can I look it up?"

First, guess at the spelling. Is it in the dictionary? If you don't see **howce** there, think of another way to write the **ow** sound. Try **houce**. If you still don't see it, think of another way to write the **soft c** sound. Try **house**.

How to say a word

"I've seen that word before, but what does it sound like?"

After the word is spelled, you'll see symbols that tell you short and long vowels and basic consonant sounds.

It also shows the syllables.

enough (ē nŭf´)

How to learn a word's meanings

"I can read the word, but how do I use it?"

After showing how to say the word, you'll see what it means. If you look up a word that sounds the same as another word, check the meaning to see if you have the right word.

kind (kīnd)

1. nice 2. a type or group

Spelling Strategies
Making Memory Clues

Even if you know every spelling rule, you just have to remember how to spell some words. Making up your own memory clue can be helpful and fun!

Write a rhyming sentence.

This memory clue helps you remember that **climb** has a **silent b** in it.

Be silent and tall as you clim**b** the wall.

Write an acrostic.

The first letter of each word spells **ocean**.

otters
can
eat
all
night

Write a silly sentence.

All the **a**'s remind you that **taught** has an **a** in it.

Annie t**a**ught **a**nts to d**a**nce.

Answer Key

Page 12

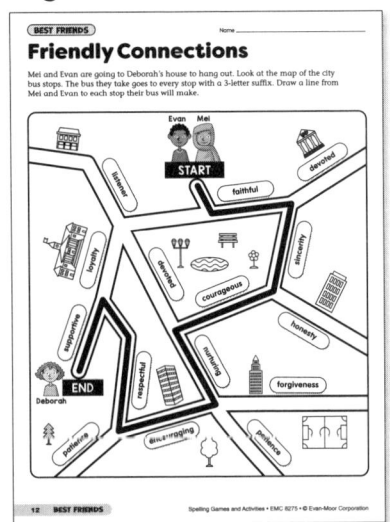

Page 13

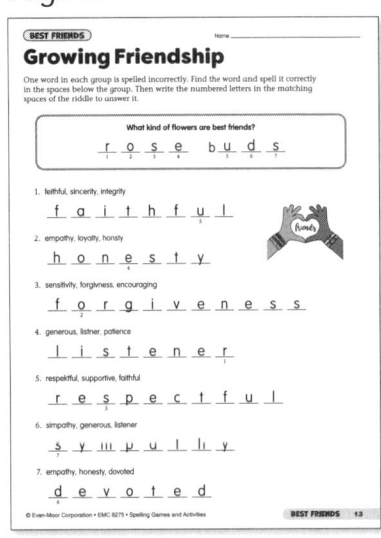

Page 14

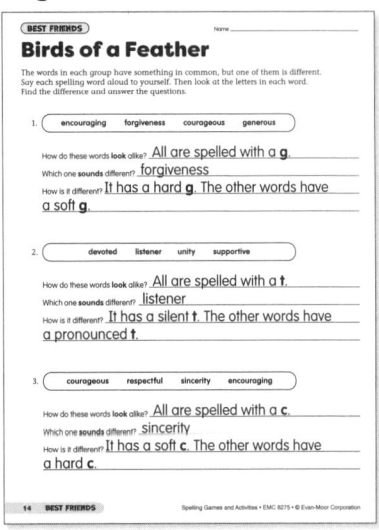

Page 15

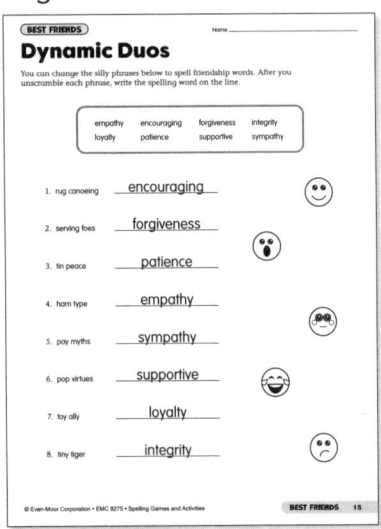

Page 16

Page 17

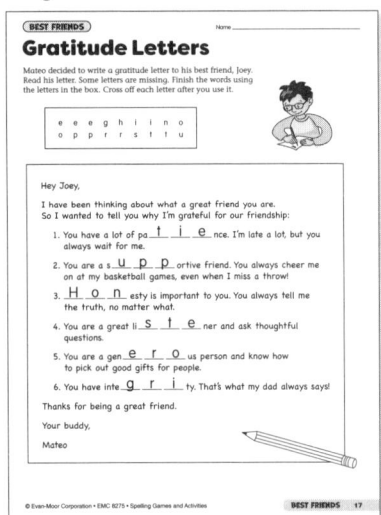

Page 22
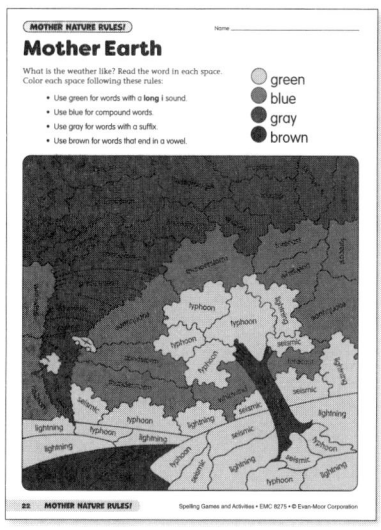

Page 23
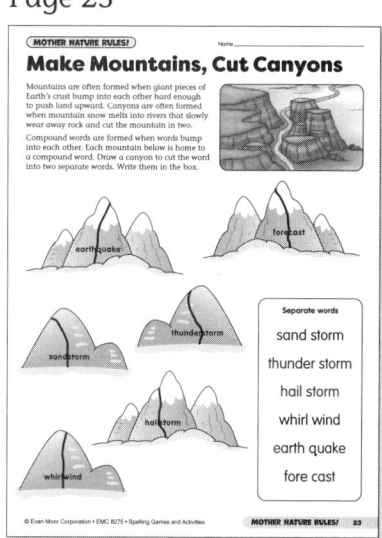

Page 24
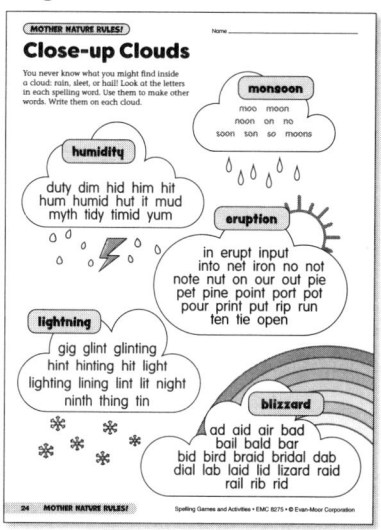

Page 25
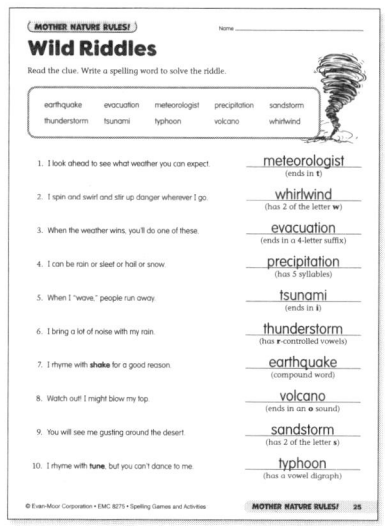

Page 26
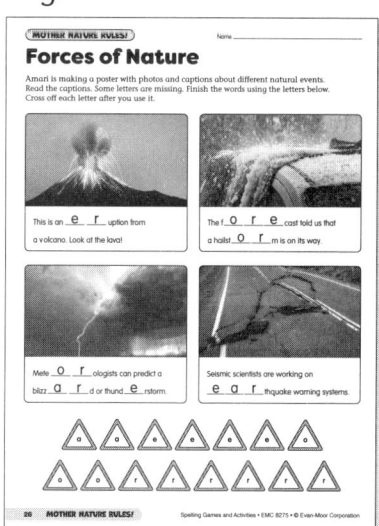

Page 27

Page 32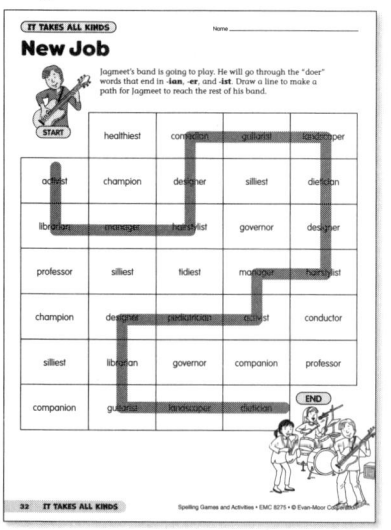

Page 33

Page 34

Page 35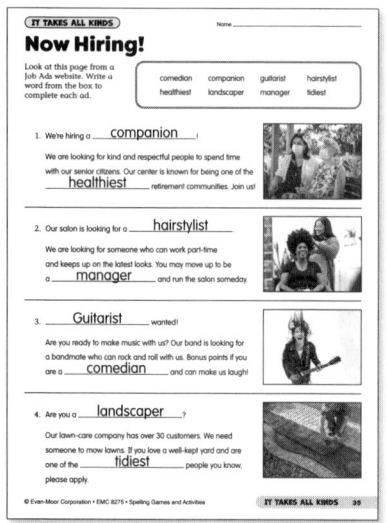

Page 36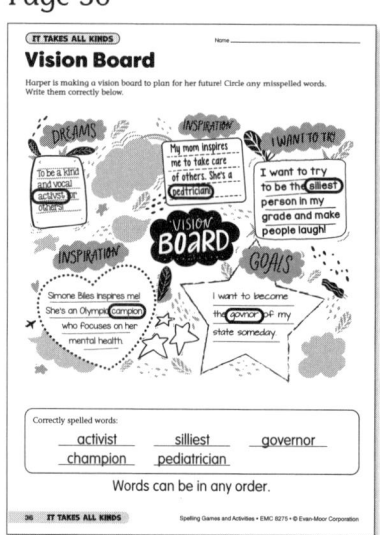

Page 37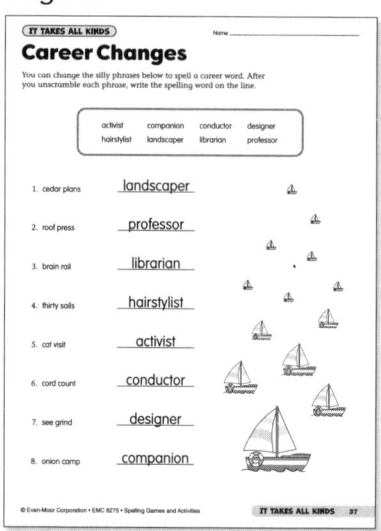

Page 42
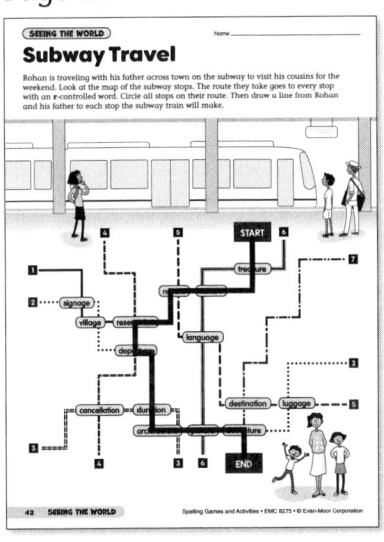

Page 43
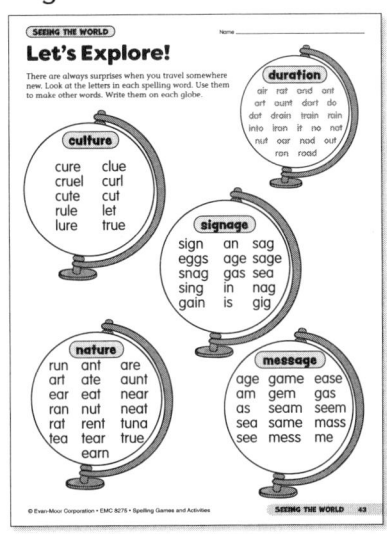

Page 44
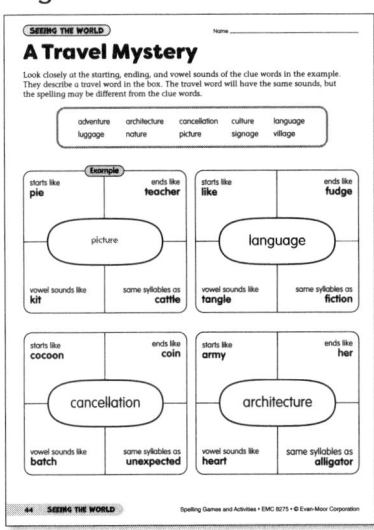

Page 45
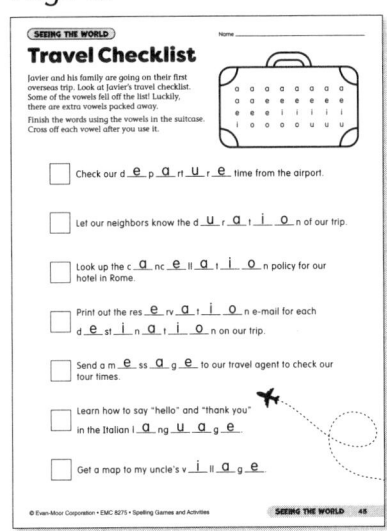

Page 46

Page 47
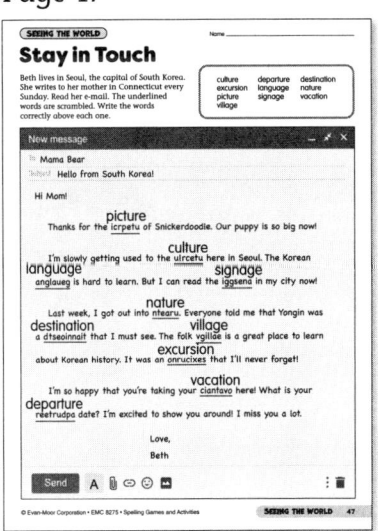

Page 52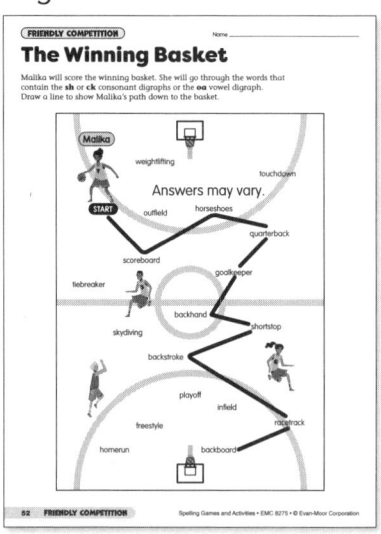

Page 53

Page 54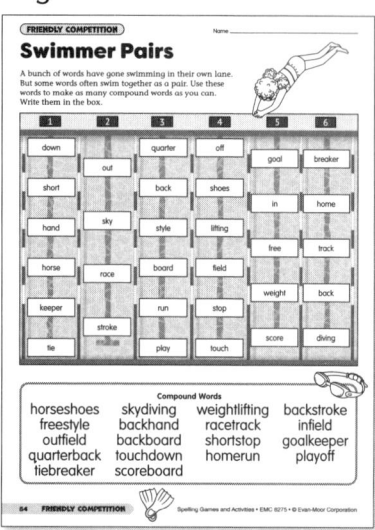

Page 55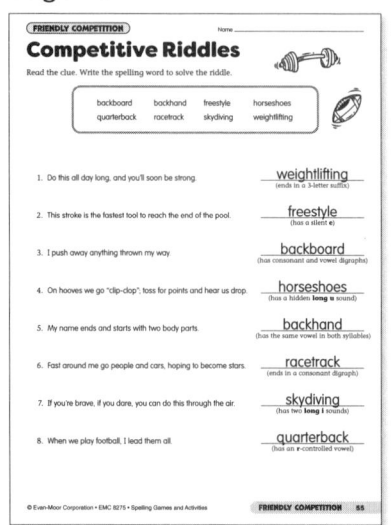

Page 56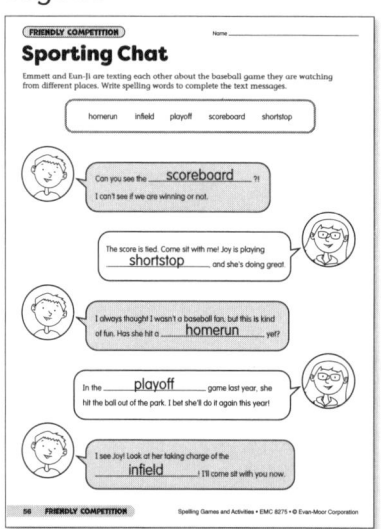

Page 57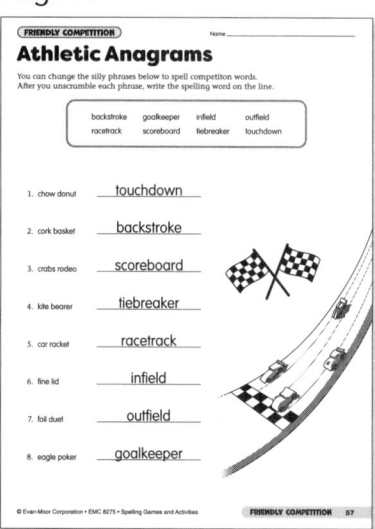

Page 62
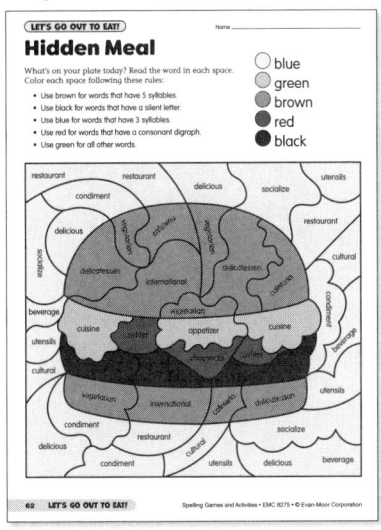

Page 63

Page 64
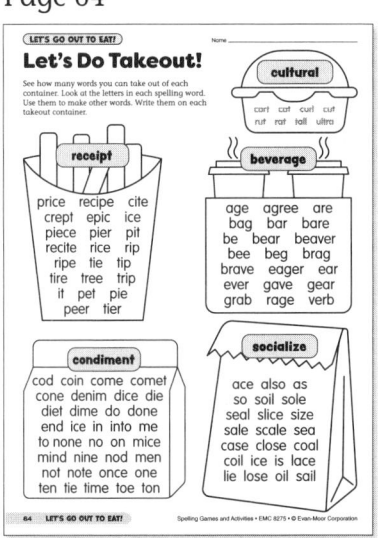

Page 65
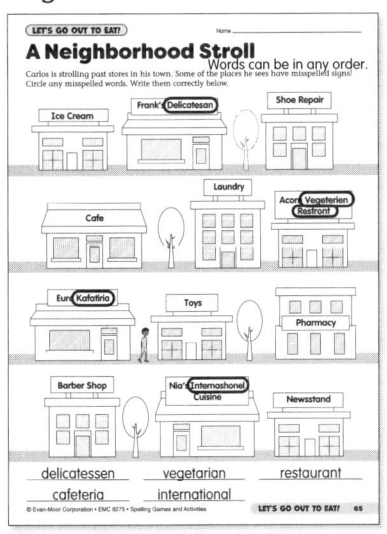

Page 66
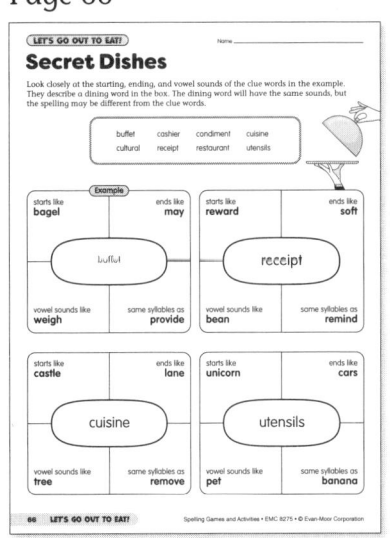

Page 67

Page 72
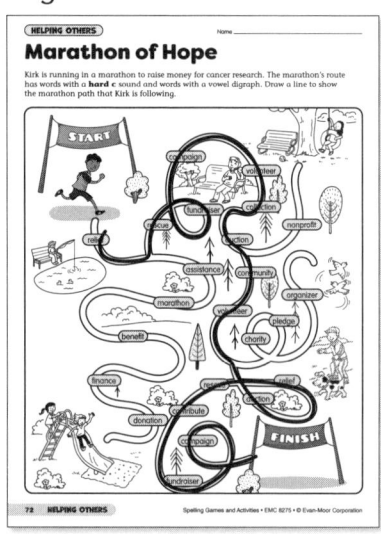

Page 73
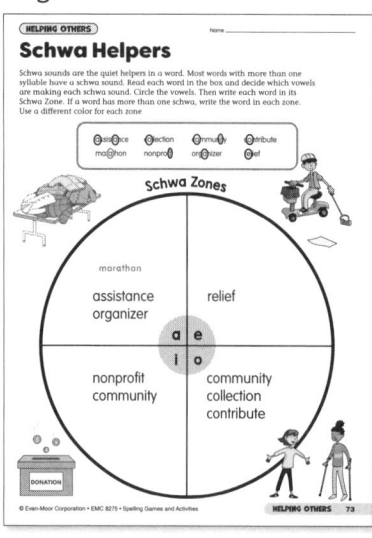

Page 74

Page 75
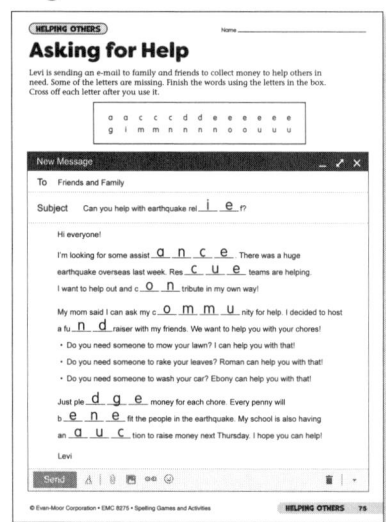

Page 76
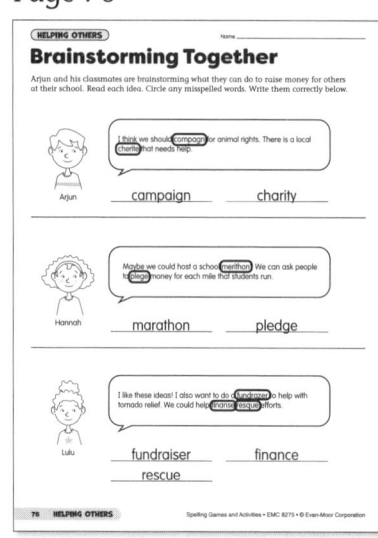

Page 77
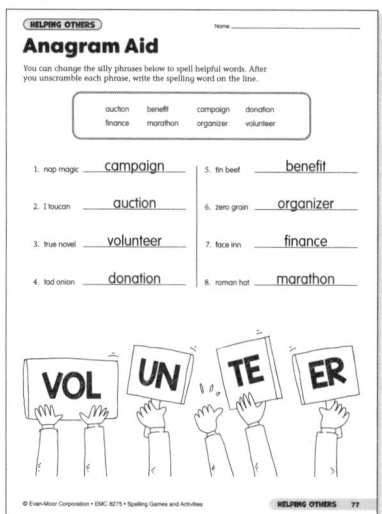

Page 82
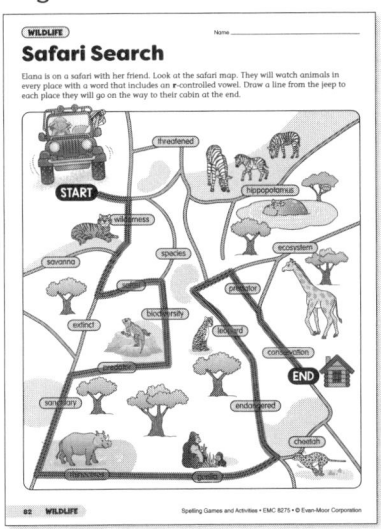

Page 83
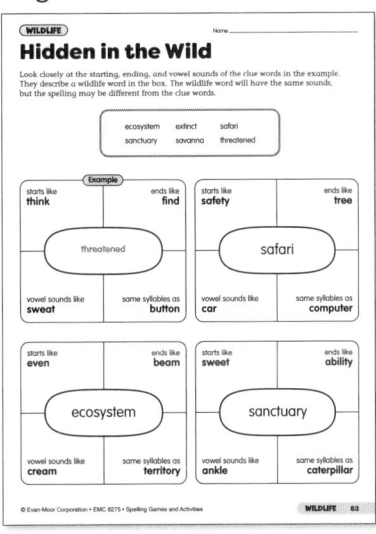

Page 84
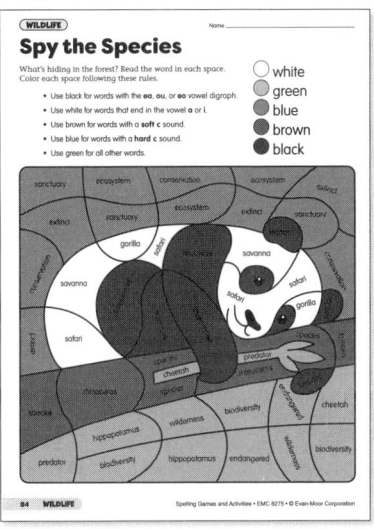

Page 85
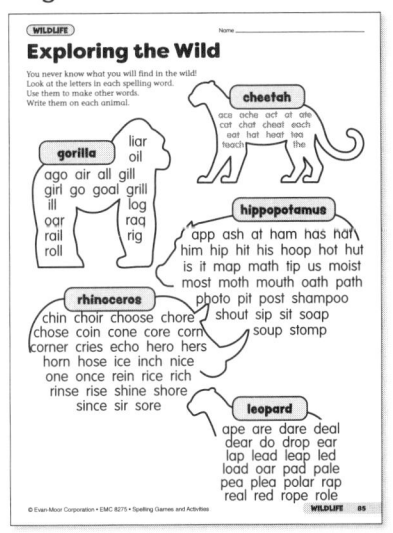

Page 86

Page 87
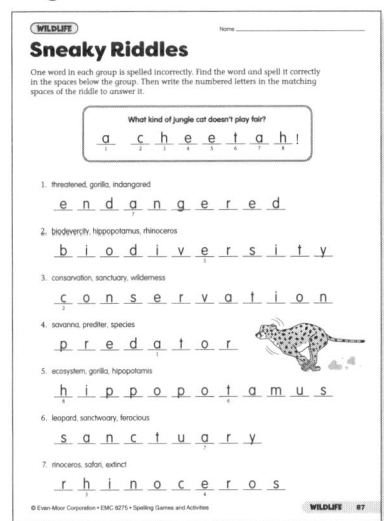

Page 92
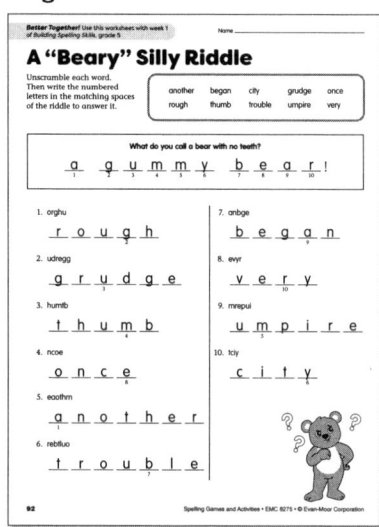

Page 93
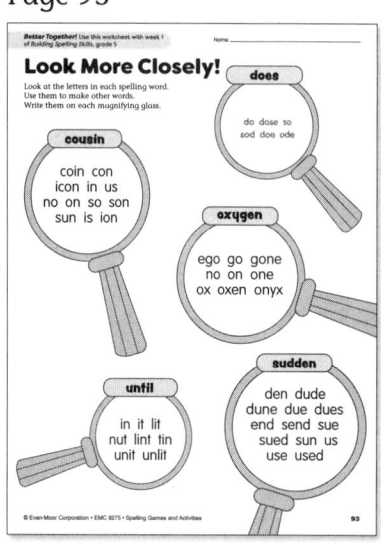

Page 94
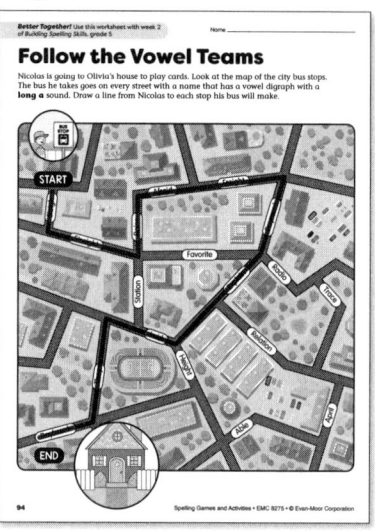

Page 95
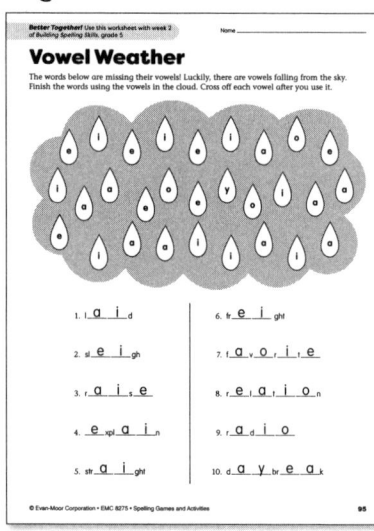

Page 96
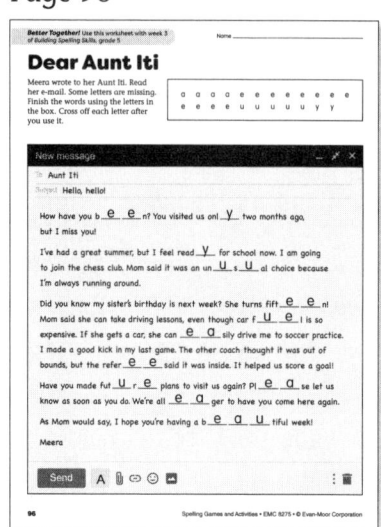

Page 97
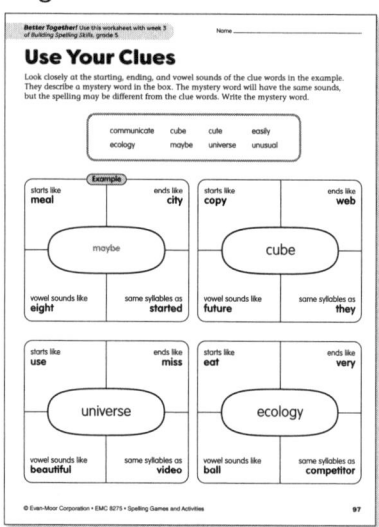

Page 98
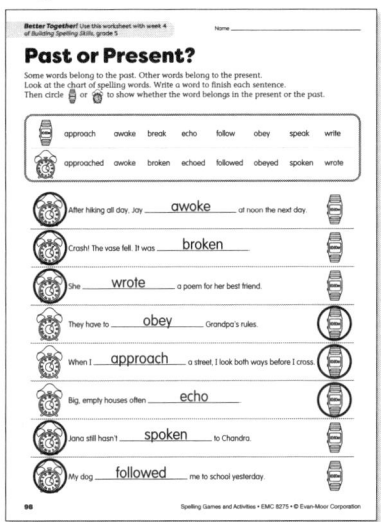

Page 99
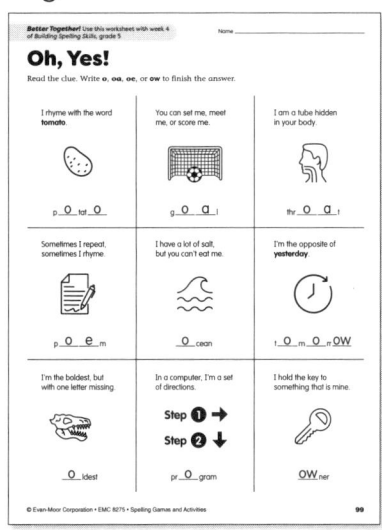

Page 100
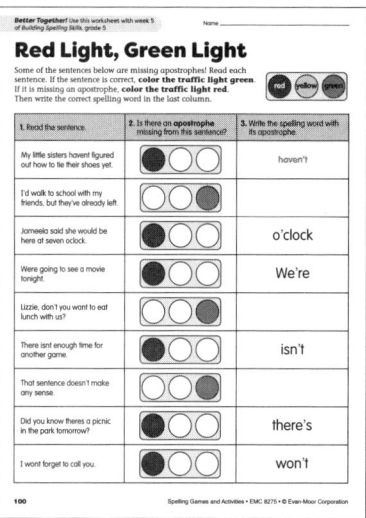

Page 101
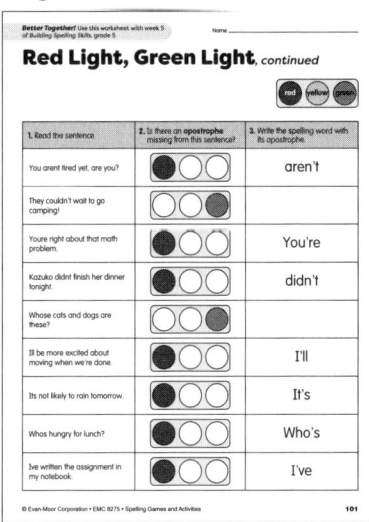

Page 102
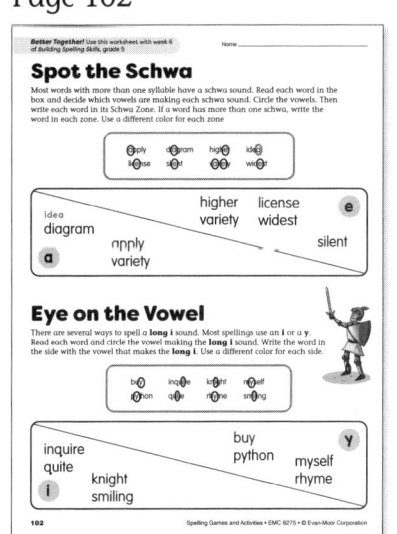

Page 103
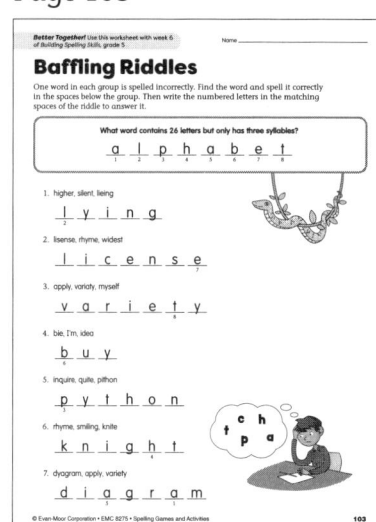

Page 104
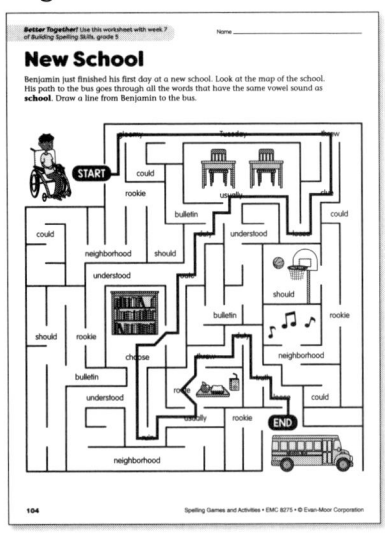

Page 105
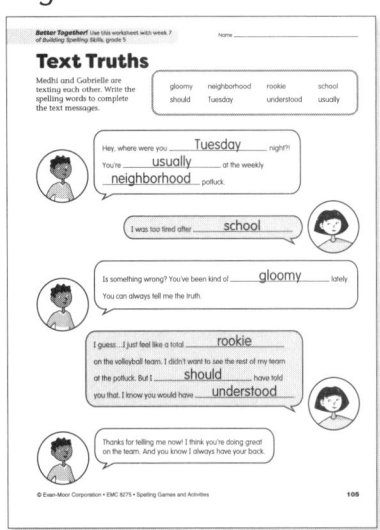

Page 106
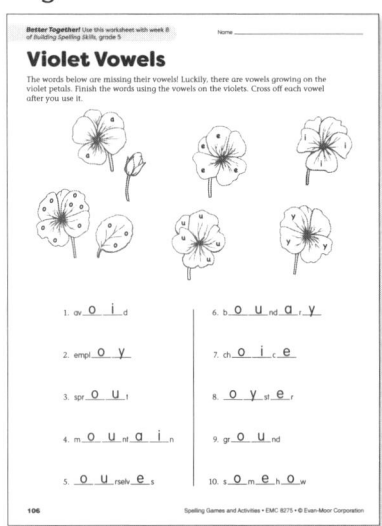

Page 107
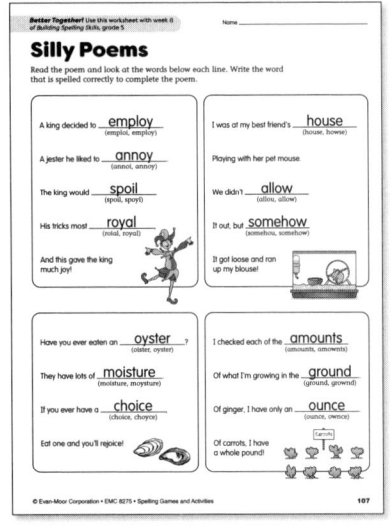

Page 108

Page 109
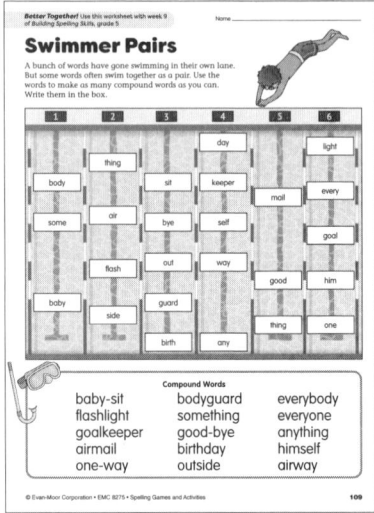

Page 110
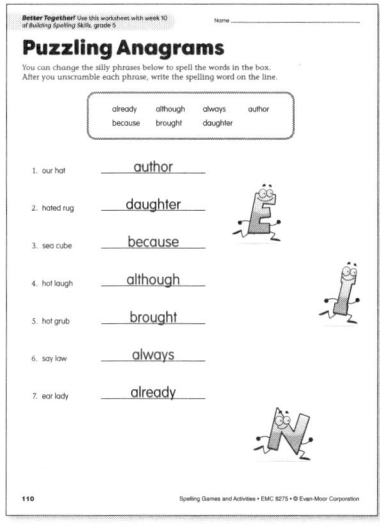

Page 111
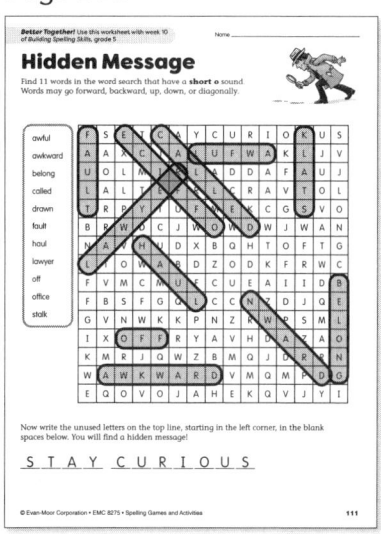

Page 112
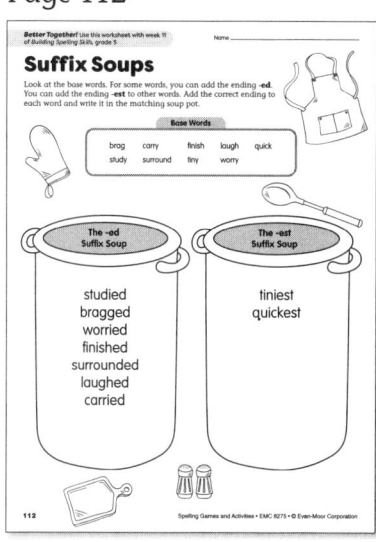

Page 113
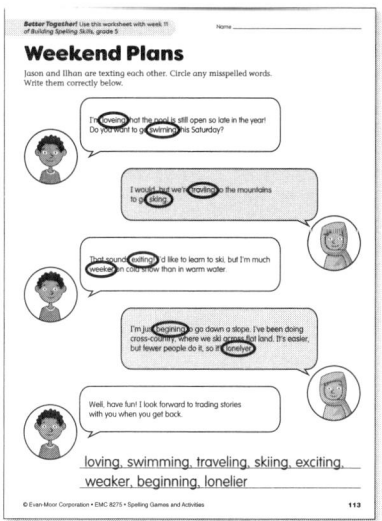

Page 114
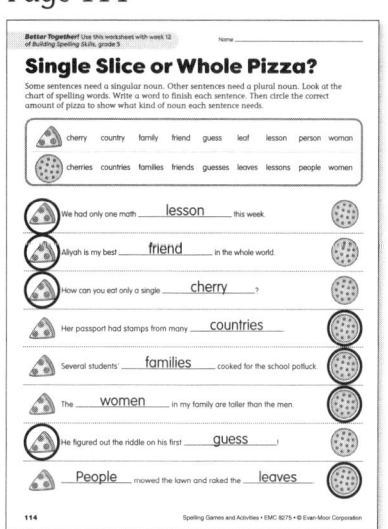

Page 115
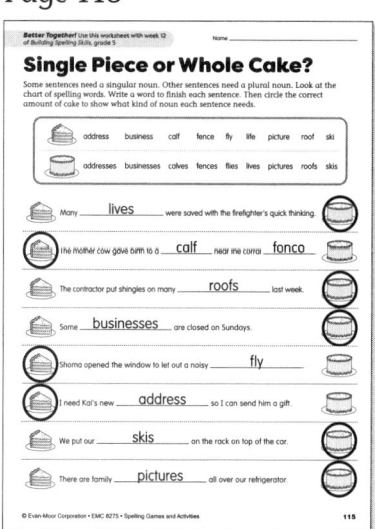

Page 116

Page 117
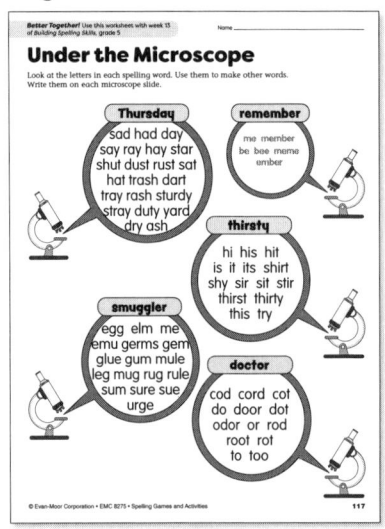

Page 118
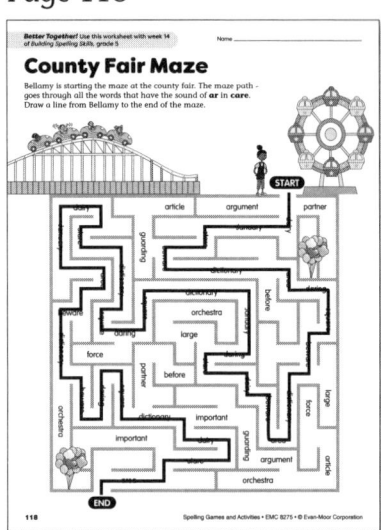

Page 119

Page 120
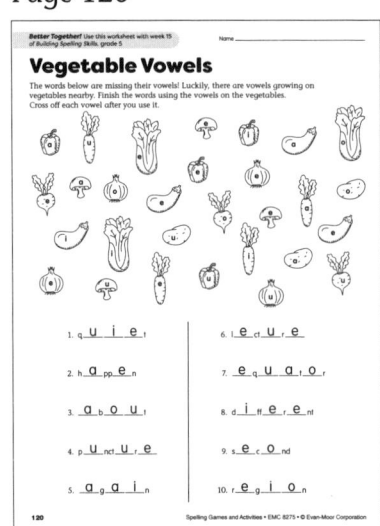

Page 121
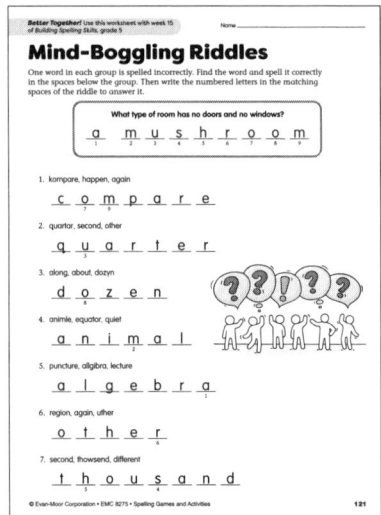

Page 122
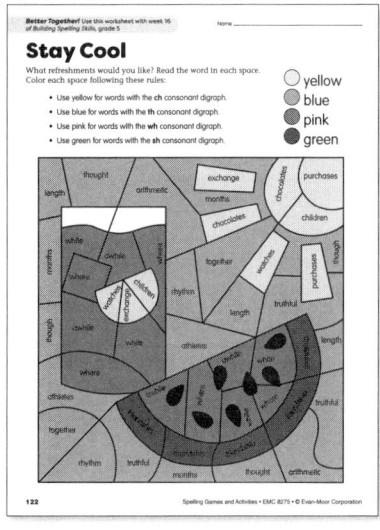

Page 123
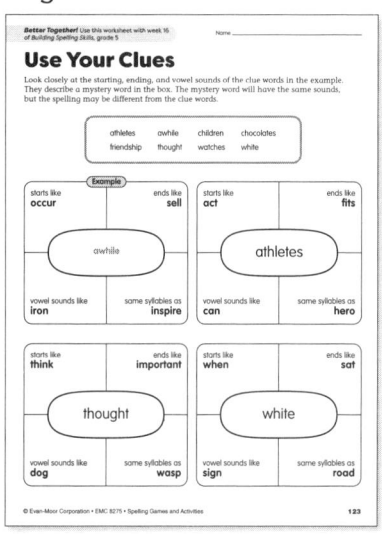

Page 124
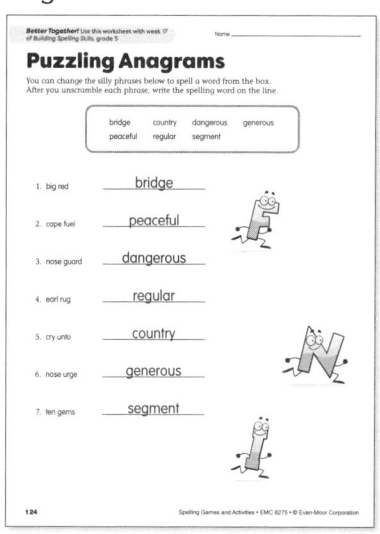

Page 125
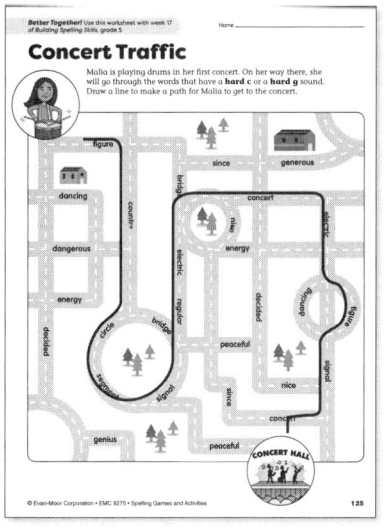

Page 126
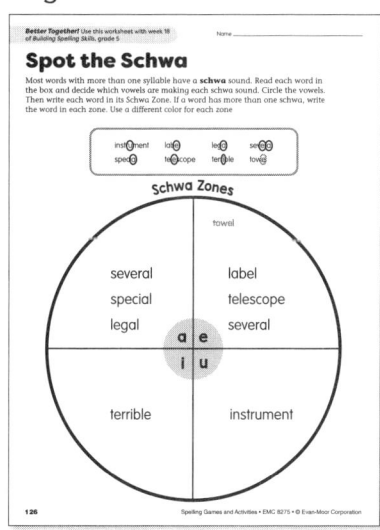

Page 127
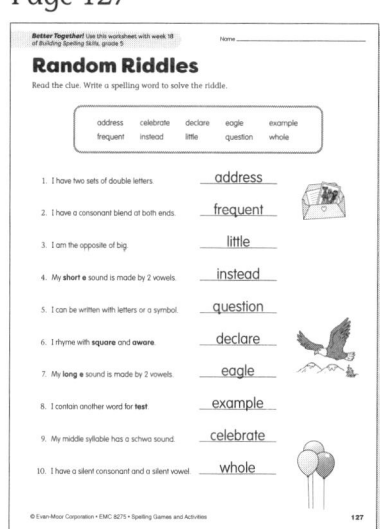

Page 128
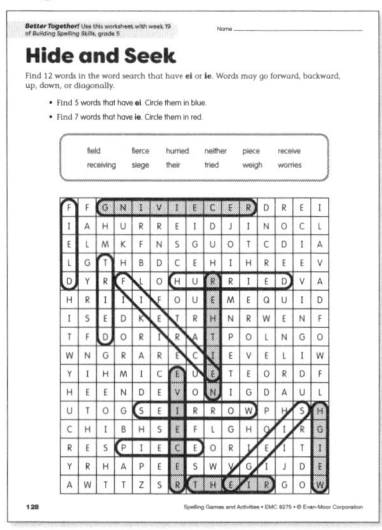

Page 129
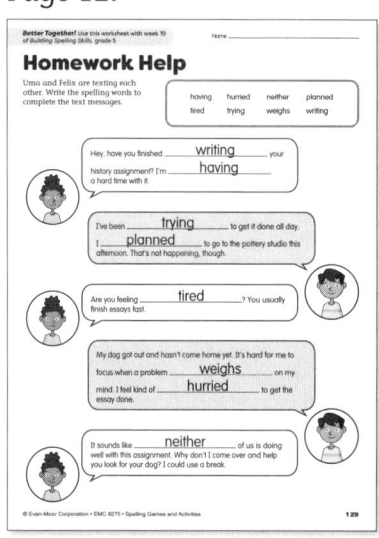

Page 130

Page 131
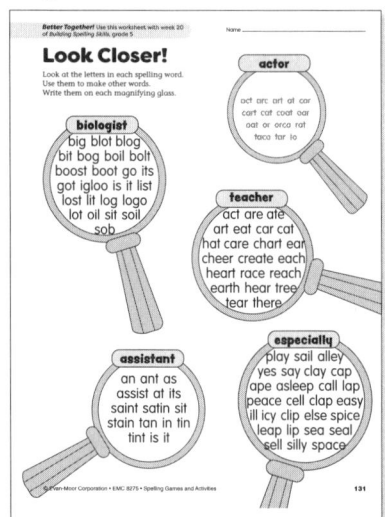

Page 132
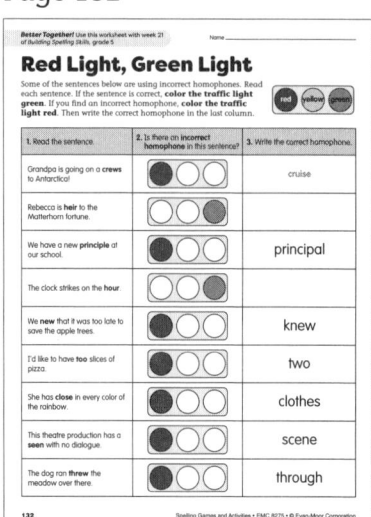

Page 133
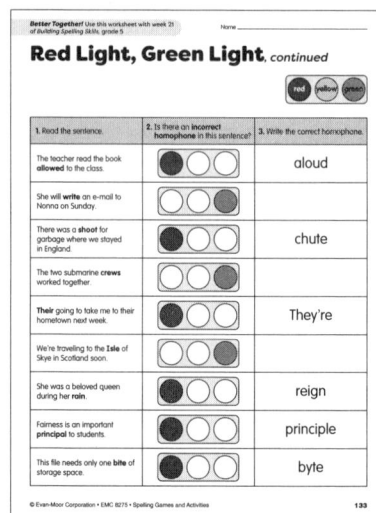

Page 134
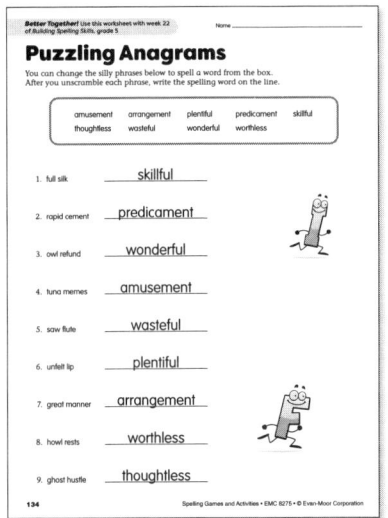

Page 135
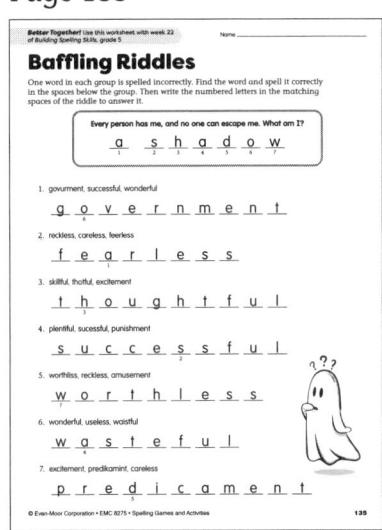

Page 136
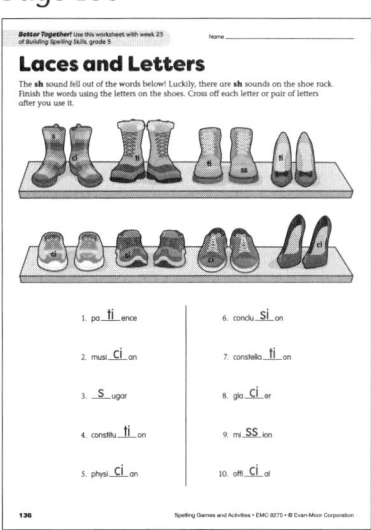

Page 137
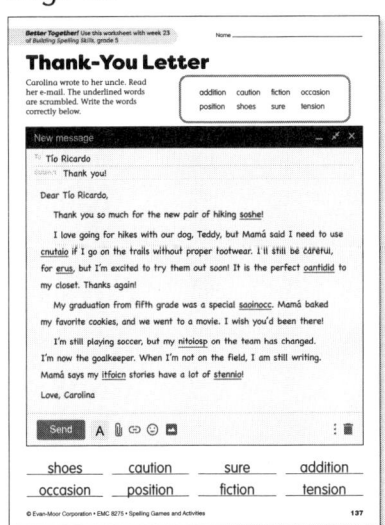

Page 138

Page 139

Page 140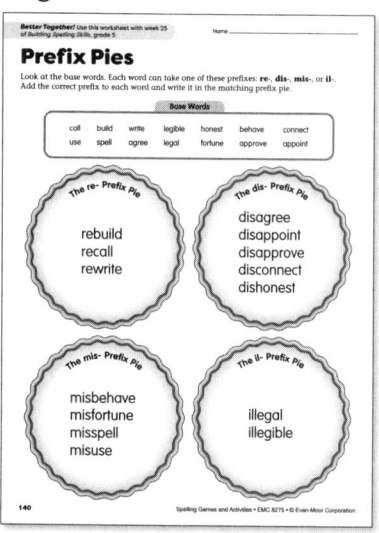

Page 141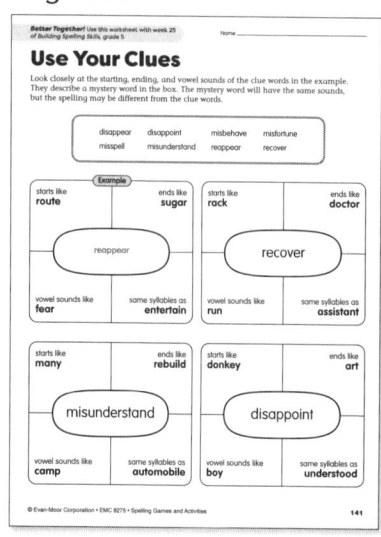

Page 142

Page 143

Page 144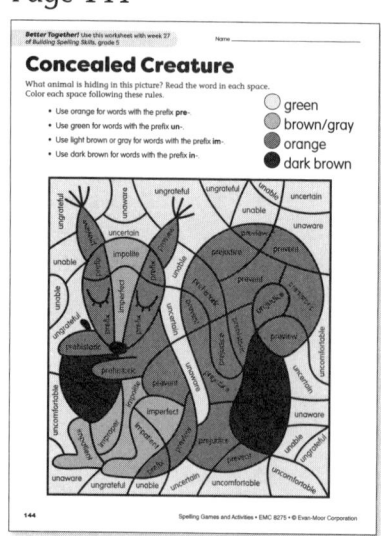

Page 145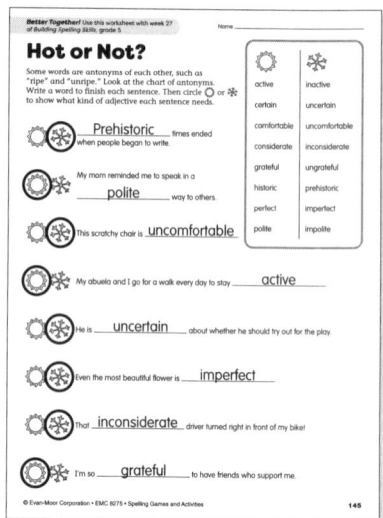

Page 146

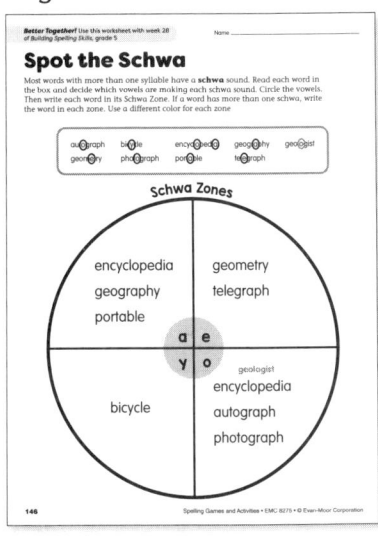

Page 147

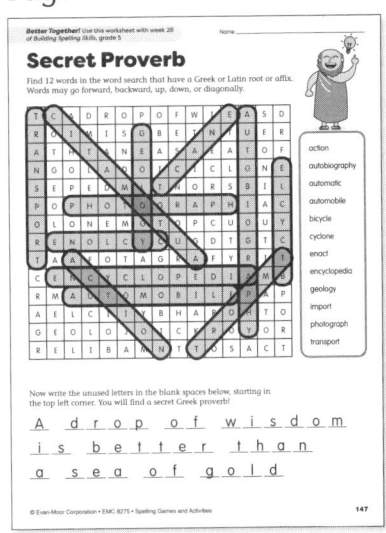

Page 148

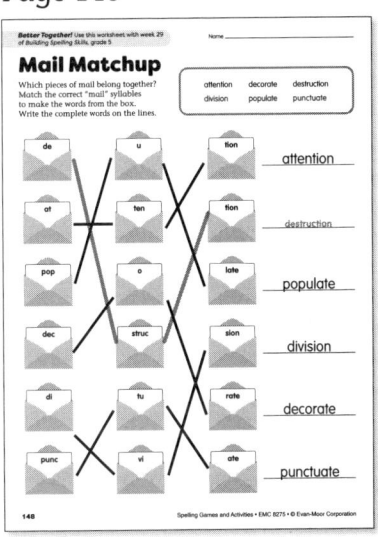

Page 149

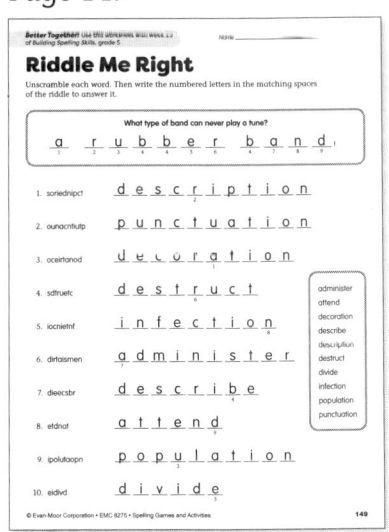

Page 150

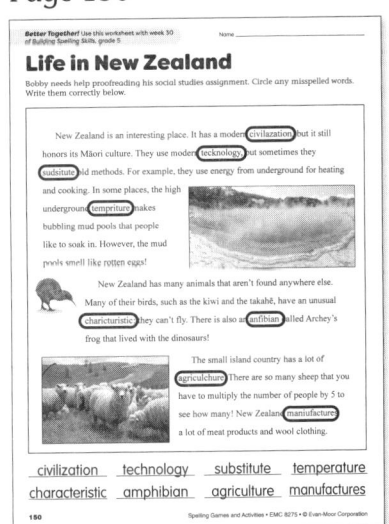

Page 151

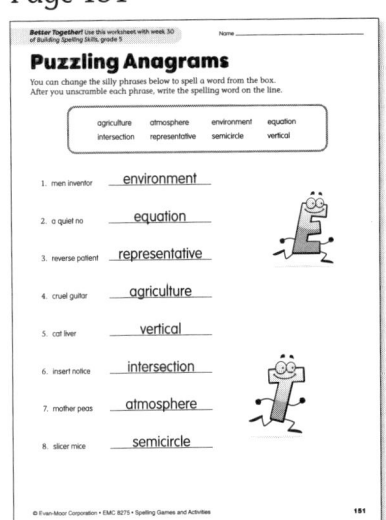